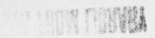

Thomas Hardy from
Serial to Novel

Thomas Hardy from Serial to Novel

By

Mary Ellen Chase

NEW YORK

RUSSELL & RUSSELL · INC

1964

TO

Edith Lord Chase

AND

Newton Kimball Chase

FOREWORD

WITH many readers of belles-lettres "research" has a bad name. It is always gratifying to the professor to have evidence that the most conscientious technical study of literature may be made to throw light on fundamental aesthetic problems. Miss Chase's work is a case in point. Any one interested in Hardy will be interested — if not positively excited — to learn what compromises this great artist was ready to make with the views of editors, — editors indifferent to considerations of artistic integrity and solely concerned not to give offense in the family circle. When all the bearings of the matter are taken, it is seen to amount to something more than a study in Hardy's literary methods. It is highly illuminating with regard to the professional ethics of editors and the general attitude of even late-Victorian England towards a consistent view of truth. When we consider what writer it was who got himself involved in this system of shifts and evasions, we have some intimation of why it is that our English fiction makes, in general, so sorry a showing, for profundity and seriousness, beside that of the French and the Russians. But here we enter the realm of the speculative and the disputed, and I will run no further risk of passing off my views for those of Miss Chase. Let her speak for herself.

JOSEPH WARREN BEACH

·CONTENTS

INTRODUCTION

INTRODUCTION

O F Thomas Hardy's fifteen novels twelve were
published as serials in various magazines before
they were issued in book form.[1] In the prefaces of only

[1] From A. P. Webb, *A Bibliography of the Works of Thomas
Hardy*, I gather the material for this list of the novels published
serially, together with the dates of book publication:

"A Pair of Blue Eyes," in *Linsley's Magazine*, Sept., 1872, to July,
1873. Date of book publication, 1873.

"Far from the Madding Crowd," in the *Cornhill Magazine*, Jan. to
Dec., 1874. Date of book publication, 1874.

"The Hand of Ethelberta," in the *Cornhill Magazine*, July, 1875,
to May, 1876. Date of book publication, 1876.

"The Return of the Native," in *Belgravia*, Jan. to Dec., 1878. Date
of book publication, 1878.

"The Trumpet Major," in *Good Words*, Jan. to Dec., 1880. Date
of book publication, 1880.

"A Laodicean," in *Harper's Monthly* (European ed.), Dec., 1880, to
Dec., 1881. Date of book publication, 1881.

"Two on a Tower," in *Atlantic Monthly*, 1882, vols. 49 and 50.
Date of book publication, 1882.

"The Mayor of Casterbridge," in the *Graphic*, Jan. 2, to May 15,
1886. Date of book publication, 1886.

"The Woodlanders," *Macmillan's Magazine*, May, 1886, to April,
1887. Date of book publication, 1887.

"Tess of the D'Urbervilles," in the *Graphic*, July 4, to Dec. 26,
1891. Date of book publication, 1891.

"The Well-Beloved," in the *Illustrated London News*, under title
"The Pursuit of the Well-Beloved," Oct. 1, 1892, to Dec. 17, 1892.
Date of book publication, 1897.

"Jude the Obscure," in *Harper's Monthly* (European ed.), Dec.,
1894, under title of "The Simpletons," Jan. to Nov., 1895, under
title "Hearts Insurgent." Date of book publication, 1896.

four of these does Hardy give us any suggestion that the serial forms differed from the later book editions. These four are *The Mayor of Casterbridge*, which was published as a serial in the London *Graphic*, from January 2 to May 15, 1886, and in book form by Smith, Elder and Company of London, probably later in the same year, no more definite date being given; *Tess of the D'Urbervilles*, which was also a *Graphic* serial, running in that magazine from July 4 to December 26, 1891, and which in the same year was issued in book form by Osgood, M'Ilvaine and Company, London, the explanatory note to the first edition being dated November, 1891; *Jude the Obscure*, published serially in *Harper's New Monthly Magazine* (European edition) December, 1894, to November, 1895, first under the title of "The Simpletons" in the December number, and then of "Hearts Insurgent," January to November, 1895, and in book form by Osgood, M'Ilvaine and Company in 1895; and finally *The Well-Beloved*, which ran as a serial in the *Illustrated London News* from October 1 to December 17, 1892, under the title "The Pursuit of the Well-Beloved," and in book form by Osgood, M'Ilvaine and Company in 1897, the preface being dated in January of that year.

In the foreword of each of these four novels[2] occurs a statement by the author to the effect that certain

---

[2] These forewords occur in the first editions of *Tess of the D'Urbervilles, Jude the Obscure,* and *The Well-Beloved.* In the case of *The Mayor of Casterbridge,* however, the foreword is in the first Osgood-M'Ilvaine edition of 1895, no explanatory preface whatever occurring in the original Smith, Elder and Company's edition of 1886.

changes have been made either in the manuscript of the serial before it was given to the book publisher, or, as in the case of *Tess* and *Jude*, in the very first form of the story before it saw the light as a serial. It is well, I think, to quote these statements.

From *The Mayor of Casterbridge*: "The present edition of the volume contains nearly a chapter which has never yet appeared in any English copy, though it was printed in the serial issue of the tale, and in the American edition. The restoration was made at the instance of some good judges across the Atlantic, who strongly represented that the home edition suffered from the omission. Some shorter passages and names, omitted or altered for reasons which no longer exist, in the original printing of both English and American editions, have also been replaced or inserted for the first time."

From *Tess of the D'Urbervilles*: "The main portion of the following story appeared — with slight modifications — in the *Graphic* newspaper; other chapters, more especially addressed to adult readers, in the *Fortnightly Review* and the *National Observer*, as episodic sketches. My thanks are tendered to the editors and proprietors for enabling me now to piece the trunk and limbs of the novel together, and print it complete, as originally written two years ago."

From *Jude the Obscure*: "It was begun as a serial story in *Harper's Magazine* at the end of November, 1894, and was continued in monthly parts. But, as in the case of *Tess of the D'Urbervilles*, the magazine version was for various reasons abridged and modified in some degree, the present edition being the first in which the whole appears as originally written."

From *The Well-Beloved*: "The present is the first publication of this tale in an independent form; and a few chapters have been rewritten since it was issued in the periodical press in 1892."

These four statements, which were called to my attention some seven years ago by Professor Joseph Warren Beach of the University of Minnesota, provoked my interest, and I resolved to discover just what these changes were and, should they prove at all significant, to attempt to account for them. Neither Professor Beach nor I, of course, felt assured at the time I undertook the study that simply because Hardy did not suggest the presence of alterations in the other novels published serially, they were not perhaps altered. Nor did we assume that this study of but four of the novels would afford exhaustive proof of Hardy's differing methods as a writer for the magazines and as a great English realist. But we felt justified in limiting the study to the four on the grounds: (1) that the alterations were probably more significant since Hardy felt called upon to acknowledge them; (2) that these novels were the later ones of Hardy, composed after his term of apprenticeship and after his success had been assured; (3) that, frankly realistic in tone, they all contained certain scenes dealing with the irregular relations between men and women, scenes extremely naturalistic in *Tess* and *Jude*, which Hardy might have felt called upon to change because of the demands of the magazine editor.

We are not at this time, however, entirely ignorant of the remaining eight novels which were published first in serial form. Professor Beach published the result of his study of *The Return of the Native* in the *Publications of the Modern Language Association* for December, 1921, under the title "Bowdlerized Versions of Hardy," thereby adding confirmatory evidence of Hardy's practice in bowdlerizing realistic material for magazine publication. I have, since completing this study, made a comparison of the serial and the book version of *The Woodlanders* (1887), which, since it deals with the illicit love of two of the characters, I thought might show proofs of bowdlerizing in the serial version. It shows none, doubtless because the scenes, even in the book, which deal with such relations are handled so conventionally that they could not offend any magazine editor or reader. As to other alterations from serial to book, they are so few as to be negligible.

The serial forms of two of the remaining six novels, *A Pair of Blue Eyes* and *The Trumpet Major*, are inaccessible to the writer, but neither of these stories contains realistic scenes which might, in the minds of Victorian magazine editors, be objectionable. As to possible alterations in the four novels remaining, which were, as I have said, first issued in serial form, I do not know. In view of the fact, however, that the chief alterations in the four novels studied, together with

The Return of the Native, are made in the treatment of realistic or naturalistic situations, and that the remaining four present no such scenes, I think I am justified in assuming it most probable that no changes of any moment are made in them.

In June, 1918, I summarized in a Master's thesis the many and most significant alterations in the periodical version of *The Well-Beloved* before it was published in book form, with my conclusions as to the probable reasons for these alterations. I have now presented in this larger work the results of a complete and minute comparison between the magazine and the book versions of the three other stories. As I have proceeded in my investigation, I have become more and more convinced that the work I have undertaken holds real significance for the student of Hardy in the light it throws upon his methods of work, the demands and prejudices of his reading public, his ability and apparent willingness to meet those demands and prejudices, and, finally, upon his own conception of his art.

I think it well, before giving the plan of my investigation, to state briefly the means and methods employed in the making of this comparative study. For the first and basic comparison I used the serial versions, which were, fortunately for me, accessible in the Minneapolis Public Library, and the present standard American edition of the novels, published by Harper and familiar to all Hardy readers. I used this edition, partly because it was the most accessible of any, but largely because it is the edition by which Hardy has been known to readers of the last quarter of a century. In making the comparison I used a system of annotation and insertion which renders the serial form of the novels easily intelligible to anyone reading the annotated books. These books I am presenting to the library of the University of Minnesota.

It seemed wise, however, that before publishing the results of this comparison, we satisfy ourselves as to possible alterations in the earliest editions of the novels before they were taken over by Harper and Brothers in 1897. We secured a first edition of *Jude the Obscure* in this country. Upon careful examination I found it practically identical with the Harper edition, the very minor changes from English to American spelling and the substitution of one adjective for another[3] being surely insignificant. Since it proved impossible to secure in this country first editions of *The Mayor of Casterbridge* and *Tess of the D'Urbervilles*, in the summer of 1921 I made in the library of the British Museum a comparison not only between the first editions of both novels and those of Harper and Brothers, but also between the first and second (English) editions of *The Mayor of Casterbridge* and between the first and fifth (English) editions of *Tess of the D'Urbervilles*. I did find several interesting alterations, especially in the case of *The Mayor of Casterbridge*, but none significant enough to affect ma-

[3] "Waggon" to "wagon," "colour" to "color," etc. "Terrific" in Harper edition, p. 357, substituted for "terrible" in the Osgood-M'Ilvaine edition, p. 380 — very likely a mistake in type-setting.

terially my conclusions already reached. I have, therefore, when I have had occasion throughout my study to refer to any minor differences between the texts of the first and the Harper edition, used notes for that purpose. These will be found, numbered serially, at the end of each chapter. Otherwise it will be understood, unless specifically stated to the contrary, that the study is based upon the original comparison between the London serials and the novels in the Harper edition.

As to the plan of the study: Proceeding chronologically, I have treated each novel, in its relation to the serial version, in a chapter by itself: first, *The Mayor of Casterbridge*; second, *Tess of the D'Urbervilles*; third, *Jude the Obscure*. In each chapter I have presented the major changes — those in incident and plot; those in characterization; those in setting, and the minor changes; those evidenced in certain additions and alterations, many of which were made obviously to improve the literary atmosphere; and finally the changes in diction and in sentence structure. I have then, in a fourth chapter, given my conclusions as to the reasons for and the significance of these alterations.

I have found of great assistance in my work two bibliographical manuals.[4] I have included also, at the close of the volume, a bibliography of books and

[4] A. P. Webb, *A Bibliography of the Works of Thomas Hardy* (London, 1916). F. Outwin Saxelby, *A Thomas Hardy Dictionary* (London, 1911).

articles which have been stimulating and helpful in the writing of the final chapter.

I am indebted to the staff of reference librarians of the Minneapolis Public Library for many courtesies shown to me during the months I worked in the reference room, and to Miss Gratia Countryman, the librarian, for permission to enter the stacks. I am especially indebted to Professor Joseph Warren Beach, the advisor of my graduate study at the University of Minnesota, for his never failing interest in this work and for his helpful encouragement and confidence.

MARY ELLEN CHASE

MINNEAPOLIS
 JUNE, 1927

THE MAYOR OF CASTERBRIDGE

THE MAYOR OF CASTERBRIDGE

SINCE there is given no more definite date than 1886 for the publication of the first edition of *The Mayor of Casterbridge*, and since Hardy himself makes no statement, as he does in the prefaces of *Tess of the D'Urbervilles* and *Jude the Obscure*, as to whether the serial or the book version was first written, it is impossible to be positive as to which is the earlier. All evidence, however, points toward the serial as the first form of the story. It was concluded in the *Graphic*, May 15, 1886, a date which would leave plenty of time for revision before book publication in the same year. Moreover, there are other proofs which, it seems to me, should be regarded as conclusive. There are evident in the first edition of the novel, as well as in the Harper edition, a great many improvements made in the diction of the serial; there are also sentences which have been obviously reconstructed for greater coherence or emphasis. These would seem unquestionably to point toward the serial as the first form of the story. There are also several passages in the serial which are not only unnecessary to the plot, but which seem to retard the movement of the story. These are omitted in the book. Finally the characters, notably those of Farfrae and Elizabeth Jane, are so strengthened in delineation in the book version as almost in themselves to verify the assumption of the revision and consequent improvement of the serial before it was republished in book form.

CHANGES IN INCIDENT AND PLOT

It is quite necessary, and, I think, not unreasonable to assume at the beginning of this chapter that the reader is familiar with the story of this first novel under discussion as that story is told in the present American edition. I am, however, summarizing the main incidents of the plot, both because such a summary will readily present the material in question, and also because, by placing an asterisk (*) before those incidents most significant to this study, I can make evident at a glance just where the main differences between the plot of the serial and that of the book occur.

The main incidents of the story, then, in the edition familiar to all are as follows:

1. Michael Henchard, intoxicated, sells his wife and child at Weydon Priors fair to a sailor named Newson.

2. He vows to drink no liquor for twenty years, and during those years rises to wealth and power in Casterbridge.

3. His wife returns, eighteen years after her sale, with her daughter Elizabeth Jane, Newson having been reported drowned.

4. Donald Farfrae arrives in Casterbridge, and,

importuned by Henchard, becomes his business manager.

*5. Complication is afforded by Henchard's previous intimate relationship with a woman in Jersey, to whom he writes explaining matters, and to whom he sends consolation money.

6. Henchard remarries his former wife.

7. Henchard grows jealous of Farfrae's growing influence in the business and social life of Casterbridge, and commands him to cease his attentions to Elizabeth Jane.

*8. Lucetta, the Jersey woman, writes for her letters to Henchard, who carries them to her coach as she is about to pass through Casterbridge, but who fails to find her.

9. Mrs. Henchard dies, and Henchard tells Elizabeth Jane that she is his daughter and not Newson's.

10. Henchard discovers a letter from his wife which discloses the stupendous fact that his daughter died in infancy, and that this Elizabeth Jane is Newson's child.

11. Henchard makes life unbearable for the innocent Elizabeth Jane, who, distressed at his treatment, becomes companion to the Jersey woman, come to Casterbridge, now that Henchard's wife is dead, to claim his former promise of marriage.

12. Farfrae and Lucetta fall in love.

13. Henchard buys corn on the advice of a weather prophet, and loses all.

*14. Henchard overhears Farfrae's proposal to Lucetta, and, going to her later, threatens to reveal their past intimacy unless she marries him.

15. The furmity-woman of Weydon Priors fair, arrested in Casterbridge, tells of his sale of his wife and child, which story causes Henchard's social ostracism.

*16. Henchard saves Lucetta and Elizabeth Jane from a savage bull, and learns from Lucetta that she is married to Farfrae.

*17. Henchard, now in the employ of Farfrae, finds in his old safe (now Farfrae's) the letters of Lucetta, who has again asked him for them, and reads them aloud to Farfrae, who suspects nothing.

*18. Lucetta meets Henchard by appointment and secures from him a promise of the letters.

19. The messenger to whom he entrusts the letters is angry at Lucetta, and reads the letters aloud in a disreputable inn of Mixen Lane.

20. Henchard, forbidden by Farfrae to take part in the celebration accorded a Royal Personage, wrestles with Farfrae but will not kill him.

21. The Mixen Lane inhabitants stage a "skimmity-ride," in which they take through the streets on a donkey the images of Henchard and Lucetta, and which proves the death of Lucetta.

22. Elizabeth Jane returns to Henchard to care for him.

23. Newson returns, is told by Henchard that Elizabeth Jane is dead, and goes away again.

*24. Henchard, having seen Newson again, leaves Casterbridge. Newson returns, Elizabeth Jane learns all, and feels resentment toward Henchard.

*25. Henchard returns to Elizabeth Jane's wedding with a gift for her, but is reproved by Elizabeth Jane and leaves.

26. Henchard dies, tended only by Abel Whittle, a half-witted former workman of his, and his body is discovered by Farfrae and Elizabeth Jane who have gone in search of him.

Such are the complicating events which form the plot of *The Mayor of Casterbridge*. How many of them are portrayed differently in the serial version of the novel, and in what do those differences consist? For, in spite of the author's announcement in his preface, which would surely lead one to expect few alterations, the changes from serial to book, in incident and plot alone, are many and significant.

The first and most important occurs in the treatment of incident five — the complication afforded by Henchard's previous intimate relationship with a woman in Jersey. In chapter xii of the standard edition,[1] the situation is treated in this wise: Henchard confides in Donald Farfrae, telling him of the sale of his wife and child, of his attempts to find them, of his oath to drink no strong liquors for twenty years, of his solitary life and rise to influence and wealth, of the return of his wife that very morning, and finally of his relationship with the woman in Jersey, whither he had gone fre-

quently on business. This relationship is described in
no uncertain terms:

". . . one autumn when stopping there I fell quite ill,
and in my illness I sank into one of those gloomy fits I sometimes suffer from, on account o' the loneliness of my domestic
life. . . . While in this state I was taken pity on by a
woman — a young lady I should call her, for she was of good
family, well bred, and well educated — the daughter of some
harum-scarum military officer who had got into difficulties, and
had his pay sequestrated. . . . This young creature was
staying at the boarding-house where I happened to have my
lodgings; and when I was pulled down she took upon herself
to nurse me. From that she got to have a foolish liking for me.
Heaven knows why, for I wasn't worth it. But being together
in the same house, and her feelings warm, we got naturally
intimate. I won't go into particulars of what our relations
were. It is enough to say that we honestly meant to marry.
There arose a scandal, which did me no harm, but was of
course ruin to her. . . . At last I was well and came
away. When I was gone, she suffered much on my account,
and didn't forget to tell me so in letters one after another; till,
latterly, I felt I owed her something, and thought that, as I had
not heard of Susan for so long, I would make this other one
the only return I could make, and ask her if she would run the
risk of Susan being alive (very slight as I believed) and marry
me, such as I was. She jumped for joy, and we should no
doubt soon have been married — but, behold, Susan appears!" [2]

In the serial story the confidential talk with Farfrae
is described in words practically identical with those of
the book until the complicating situation arises. But
with that situation and in the handling of it comes a

decided change. The account from the serial speaks for itself:

"Well, this summer I was there, and met with an accident. I fell out of a boat in the harbour, and struck my head in falling. If somebody had not helped me instantly, I should have been drowned. An account of it was in our local newspapers at the time."

"Indeed. And it's all haphazard in this life!"

"But the account was not complete. The person who saved me was a woman — a merchant's daughter — a woman who — God knows why, for I never gave her encouragement! — who has had a foolish liking for me more than five years; ever since I first knew her from going over there to deal with her father. So when I found I owed my life to her, in a moment of gratitude and excitement I offered to marry her. I did marry her — I married her at St. Heliers a fortnight ago. Three days after I came home here to get the house ready for her, and await her coming. But from the moment I landed, I felt I had acted rashly. It was not that I dreamed of Susan living; but I felt I did not care for this young woman, much as she might like me. Odd as it may seem to you, I've always liked Susan in my heart, and like her best now. Well, now Susan has returned to life, and you begin to see the color o't; for the other is coming by the packet tomorrow night." Henchard's voice grew brokenly indicative of passionate revolt against eighteen years of caution. "I've compromised myself by acting a fortnight too soon!" [3]

The differences here are too evident to need summarizing. The most significant is, obviously, in Henchard's relations with the woman: in the book, those relations are "intimate"; in the serial, there is no suggestion of intimacy before marriage. In fact, Henchard offers to marry the woman "in a moment of gratitude and excitement." He is, most evidently, not carried away by passion, for from the moment he lands in England, he feels not only that he has acted rashly, but that he does not "care for this young woman." Quite apparently either Hardy, or the editor of the London *Graphic*, or both, thought it wiser to depict the conventional love affair, rather than the unconventional, for their Victorian readers.

It is hardly necessary to comment upon the fact that the details of the serial version of the affair are far more sensational than those of the book. Surely to fall out of a boat in the harbor, to strike one's head in falling, and to be saved by a woman from drowning afford greater dramatic effect than merely to fall "quite ill." And if the marriage in itself sacrifices to a sense of propriety much of the interest always engendered by an irregular love affair, that sacrifice is atoned for in a large measure, at least to the magazine reader, by the melodramatic situation of the other woman's impending arrival upon the scene.

This new complication announced by Henchard, "the other is coming by the packet tomorrow night," makes necessary the addition of other material to the serial version of the story. The woman, arriving on the packet-boat, must not be allowed to enter upon a scene already sufficiently dramatic by the return of Susan Henchard. Thus it is that, whereas in the book Henchard, after telling Farfrae his story, accepts the latter's advice and writes the woman in Jersey, enclosing a check for consolation money, in the serial we find the addition of considerable material, motivated obviously by the imminent appearance of the other woman.

The following passages from the serial explain themselves. The first follows almost immediately upon Henchard's announcement that the woman is arriving the next evening.[4] The second comes at the conclusion of chapter xii, which chapter in the book concludes with Henchard's mailing of the letter, and in the serial with the passage under consideration.[5]

First passage:

"Ye must give up the younger one, sir; and since that's the case you must write and stop her coming."

"A letter cannot reach her by post before she has started. No — somebody must meet her, and let her know all; so that she must go back by the packet which returns as soon as the other arrives. Now I feel I ought not to see her; and the question is, Will you do me the good turn of going for me?"

"Yes — I will," said Farfrae, after a moment's thought.

"You are a good fellow. Take a note — that's all you need do — leave the rest to her."

"Very well. Did ye ever tell her of the other wife's history?"

"Every word except the sale. Oh, yes, Farfrae, I wouldn't have married again without letting the woman know I had no proof of Susan's death. But you can hardly think how far we were from expecting this. Eighteen years of silence — who'd have thought it!"

Farfrae seemed much relieved to hear that Henchard had acted openly toward the unfortunate second woman; it rehabilitated him in his good opinion at once. "Ah, well, it cannot be helped!" he said with philosophic woefulness. "In your letter you must put it plain and honest that it turns out she is not your wife, the first having come back; so ye cannot see her; and that it would be wise in her to keep what has happened a secret between you for her own sake; and that ye wish her weel."

"That won't do — dammy. I must do a little more than that — I must, though she did always brag about her rich uncle, and how much he could leave her — settle something upon her, I suppose — just as a little restitution, poor girl. . . . Will ye draw up a bit of a form for me to that effect? I'm so bad at letters."

"I will."

"Luckily, owing to the recent death of her parent, she insisted upon the wedding being quiet; and now she profits by her modesty."

"Perhaps she thought, 'If I keep it dark, and his other wife comes back, I'll return to Jersey and be none the worse a maid for another husband?' "

"No, no," said Henchard, peremptorily. "She's not that sort o' body at all; more of a gushing, thoughtless nature. However, that's what I must do."[6]

Second passage:

Thus the evening ended, and the next day at dusk saw Far-frae trotting on horseback up the Budmouth road, bearing in his pocket a letter in Henchard's handwriting addressed, "Mrs. Henchard, Jersey packet-boat." It contained a fair statement of what had happened, and he had enjoined Farfrae to deliver it into her hands before she landed, by boarding the packet with the officer of customs. Then, when she had read it, to see her

on board the return boat and come away. A written promise
to pay her a good round sum as consolation money was also to
be given — this being Henchard's rough way, indeed only way,
of making amends.

The young man sped along the hard, smooth road towards
the coast. About half way he passed the top of a ridge which
formed a kind of girdle enclosing the rural districts of the
county from those shoreward. A marine sentiment in the landscape followed; there was a change in the smell of the air from
field and fruit and yellow mist to a raw discomforting breeze.
The cosiness of the inland country had gone.

In about forty minutes Farfrae stood on the quay in Budmouth harbor. The boat was fairly punctual. Farfrae immediately went on board.

There was only one lady passenger, and she was too ill to
see him just then. "Tell her I have a letter from — her husband," said Farfrae, carefully avoiding to mention names, both
on her account and Henchard's, "and I should like to deliver
it into her own hands."

The stewardess came back with the message that still the
lady could not see him for an hour, being in a disarranged state
owing to the breezy passage; but that she would receive the
letter if such were his instructions. Farfrae thereupon descended
to the cabin entrance, and in a moment or two a white hand
and arm were stretched out from behind a curtain that hung
across the door-way. He murmured, "Mrs. Henchard?" The
owner of the hand said, "Yes," and he placed the letter within
her fingers which were quickly withdrawn.

In half-an-hour he again sought the boat, to lend his assistance in shifting the unfortunate young lady to the returning
vessel. But she had already gone there. Farfrae, to tell the
truth, though pitying her, was somewhat relieved that the letter

had done its work so smoothly and promptly; and he lost no time in mounting for his homeward ride.

Henchard awaited him like a statue under the third tree of the avenue; for it was now past midnight, and no idlers remained in the roads.

"Well?" said the cornfactor.

"It is done — exactly as you said," replied the Scotchman; and he explained particulars.

Henchard was thoughtful.[7]

Comment upon these additional serial passages is hardly necessary. As I have said, they serve to solve the complication afforded by the arrival of Henchard's second wife. The second incident, which deals with Farfrae's ride to Budmouth and his delivery of the letter to the "white hand and arm . . . stretched out from behind a curtain," adds another sensational touch, probably not unpleasing to the magazine public. The Hardy reader is, however, quite conscious of the sacrifice of the author's usual conciseness in the handling of incident by the intrusion of so many more or less ill-chosen details.

Another difference in the serial story is seen in the treatment of incident eight, in which, in the book edition, Lucetta writes for her letters to Henchard, who carries them to her coach as she is about to pass through Casterbridge, but who fails to find her.[8] Lucetta's letter to Henchard, in reply to his fateful one to her (which, it will be remembered, is, in the book, mailed to her by Henchard himself; in the serial, delivered by Farfrae), is practically the same in both book and serial, except for necessary changes in certain words and the insertion or omission of certain phrases and clauses which suggest the difference in relationship depicted in the two versions — in the serial, marriage; in the book, intimacy without marriage.[9]

It is in Henchard's fulfillment of Lucetta's request for her letters that the chief difference in the handling of the situation takes place. In the book, as already stated, Henchard, informed by Lucetta's letter that she is to pass through Casterbridge on her way from Bristol to Budworth, meets the coach to deliver the letters, but finds no Lucetta. He, therefore, concluding that something has happened to change her plans, takes the letters home again and returns them to his safe. In the serial, there are two interesting, though not particularly significant, dissimilarities. The first — the meeting of Mrs. Henchard and Lucetta (which is entirely absent from the book) — is a detached incident, and seems to have no connection with the returning of the letters. It evidently serves no purpose except to present a decidedly ironical situation to the serial reader, and, perhaps, to excite suspense at the possibility of something happening. The second — the entrusting of the letters to Elizabeth Jane by Henchard, Farfrae's offer to deliver them for her (the coach being late), his failure to find the lady in question, and the subsequent failure of the guard to whom he, in turn, gives the letters — suggests a desire on the part of the author of the serial to give even added emphasis to the vicissitudes through which Lucetta's unfortunate letters must pass before they, in the end, prove her undoing. One who reads the following account of the two occurrences will, I think, be again convinced that the serial plot, though it may gain in sensationalism, is, in yet another incident, lacking in the artistic effectiveness evident in the book itself:

Mrs. Henchard sent to him from the room soon after, and he went up. "I feel so much better, Michael," she said, "that I shall go out in a chair towards the middle of the day."

Henchard arranged that the chair should be ready, and went about his daily business. About twelve o'clock he was passing round the south side of the town, outside the earthwork of the Walls; and glancing into the chestnut avenue he saw that his wife was taking the air as she had planned. Old Solomon Longways, with a long white wooden rake, was scraping together the yellow, brown, and green leaves which had fallen, and heaping them into a deep wheelbarrow; they were insinuating visitors, those autumn leaves, sailing down the air into chimneys, green-houses, and roof gutters; even finding their way, in some mysterious manner, as far as the Town Pump — that center and hub of the borough. But what attracted Henchard was other than this; it was the fact that his wife's chair was pulled up beside a lady seated on a bench at the edge of the walk — a lady closely veiled, of graceful figure, wearing a Paisley shawl with a red centre.

Upon her shoulders, and upon his wife's, an occasional red leaf rested as it floated down. They were talking after the manner of those whom a common recreation spot had made acquaintances. Henchard looked thunderstruck when he beheld the incident. Then he seemed to fancy himself mistaken, especially as the day was not the day mentioned in Lucetta's letter; and thus he went on his way.

"I saw you talking to a friend in the Walk," he said to Susan at dinner, as she sat propped up by a cushion.

"Yes," said the unwitting Mrs. Henchard. "She was a stranger to me, however. She was a kind, lady-like young woman, on her way to Bristol; and she had stopped to look at the town for half-an-hour, which she had never seen before."

Henchard sank into dumbness at this news, which reconfirmed his original conviction. He disliked the idea of that meeting, and wondered if Lucetta had aimed to see his wife, or whether the conjuncture were an accident.

Nothing occurred to enlighten him, and three days afterwards, the time she had appointed for receiving her old letters, he sealed them up in a packet which he placed in the hands of Elizabeth Jane, she being one who could execute such a commission without burning curiosity or troubling questioning. She was directed to meet the Bristol coach at the Stag Hotel, and give the parcel to a Miss St. Helier inside who should ask for such a thing. Elizabeth had not seen Lucetta, if it had been Lucetta with her mother in the Chestnut Walk, so that he thought there would be no risk worth considering.

At dusk Elizabeth Jane went and stood opposite the coach office, close to the inn yard. The evening was rather chilly and the coach happened to be late. While she stood she saw Farfrae coming round by the town pump, and he crossed over to her. Though there was no positive reason for so doing, she could not help telling him why she was waiting there. "Shall I give it to the lady? — I'll do so with pleasure if you find it tedious to stay," he said. Elizabeth accepted his offer, and came away.

The coach at last arrived, and there was nobody inside or out who asked for such a parcel. Farfrae was now rather embarrassed, till the guard declared that he knew the lady described — that she had passed through Casterbridge from Budmouth to

Bristol three or four days before, and had mentioned this time for her return. He thought she must have missed the coach, but would probably come on the following journey; he could give her the package if Farfrae would entrust him with it. The latter thereupon handed it over to him.

A fortnight afterward when Farfrae was walking along the street, the guard of the same coach came to him with the information that, though he had carried the packet up and down with him ever since, the lady had not returned; and he reproduced the article from his capacious pocket. Farfrae took the bundle, which had evidently been investigated and deemed a profitless burden. He reached home, guessed the letters were the property of the lady Henchard had become involved with, understood the plan, and was in doubt what to do. He put them aside till he should meet Miss Newson, and tell her what had occurred.[10]

The wording of incident fourteen, as given in the beginning of the chapter, is proof that there must be differences in its treatment in the serial version. "Henchard overhears Farfrae's proposal to Lucetta, and, going to her later, threatens to reveal their intimacy in Jersey unless she marries him." The differences are, however, merely the necessary changes in wording in view of the dissimilarity, already established, between the relations of Henchard and Lucetta in the serial and in the book. These changes are too slight to have any influence upon the plot, yet a summarizing of them may serve to show the care taken by Hardy in his revision of the serial, so that he might not lay himself open to the charge of inconsistency. This summarizing is best accomplished by quoting, from the Harper edition, the most significant portions of the dialogue between Henchard and Lucetta, together with the corresponding parts of the serial, which parts are enclosed in brackets. The italicized portions occur only in the book, not in the serial.

Lucetta: "Had I found that you *proposed to marry* [married] me for pure love I might have felt *bound now* [the vow binding, though it was not legal.] But I soon learnt that you had *planned* [done] it out of mere charity — almost as an unpleasant duty — because I had *nursed you, and compromised myself,* [helped save your life] and you thought you must repay me [in some way]."

Henchard: "Why did you come here to find me, then?"

Lucetta: "I thought I ought to *marry* [re-marry] you for conscience' sake. . . ."

Henchard: "[You belong to me, and] You cannot in honor refuse me. . . . And unless you give me your promise this very night to be my [legal] wife, before a witness, I'll *reveal our intimacy* [disclose all] — in common fairness to other men." [11]

The first part of incident sixteen — in which Henchard saves Lucetta and Elizabeth Jane from a savage bull — affords an interesting comparison between its treatment in the serial, on the one hand, and in the book, on the other. In itself the bull episode, in neither version, is particularly significant. It merely motivates in both the rather ironical situation of a man who, having saved the life of the woman he wants, finds she is married to someone else. But, significant or not, it gave to the author of the serial story an opportunity for a heightening of excitement and suspense, which he was not slow to seize. Thus it happens that the account of the attack by the bull in the serial version is, by the addition of the passage here quoted, given three times the space accorded to it in the later book version. A study of this additional passage, together with a comparison of minor differences in the portion common to both serial and book, will serve to show the apparent predilection on the part of the magazine reader of the eighties for the sensational:

It was possible that the impact of his horns on the stonework had caused the bull some pain, for he was more violent than ever.

"Don't turn your back to him," cried Elizabeth Jane. "We made a mistake in that. If I could get hold of the leading-stick, perhaps I could manage him."

Lucetta was too terrified to heed or hear what her younger companion said. She looked so lily-white that the other beseeched:

"Keep up, keep up, dear; and move behind me! Could you open the door if I were to draw him off his way?"

"Oh no, no! I cannot. I wish he would come! It is all over with us now!"

Elizabeth Jane being much the cooler as well as the stronger had, whilst Lucetta was speaking, by a combination of dexterity and courage, darted forward and seized the staff affixed to the bull. So accustomed had the animal been to obey the holder of that staff that for a moment — such is discipline — he seemed quite cowed, while the girl cried to Lucetta, "Climb the clover-stack." But the bull, soon finding that he was in new and fragile hands, began swaying his head this way and that, dragging Elizabeth with him as if she were a reed.

Her danger was imminent, and her sole chance lay in keeping the staff extended, while a thrust against the wall might probably have been the end of her.

"I can hold on no longer," she gasped, the hot air from her antagonist's nostrils blowing over her like a sirocco. She suddenly let go, and scrambled up the clover by a short ladder which lay half buried in the stack. Reaching the top she was comparatively safe, unless the bull should undermine the stack, which was but loosely piled. He contented himself, however, for the present with knocking down the ladder. She now looked around for Lucetta whom she believed to have gone up before her. But Lucetta was not behind her anywhere; and in a few instants, to her horror, she perceived her companion at the other and vacant end of the barn, whither she had run in her bewilderment, while Elizabeth was engaged with the animal.

The bull, too, saw Lucetta now, and depressed his horns with deliberate aim, as if he felt there was plenty of time at least to do the thing well. A rattling at the door distracted him. In a moment a man burst in, plunged toward the leading-staff, seized it, and wrenched the animal's head as if he would snap it off.[12]

The latter part of incident sixteen — in which Henchard asks Lucetta to marry him and discovers that she is already married to Farfrae — is almost identical in the diction of both versions.

Several changes from serial to book are made necessary in the treatment of incident seventeen—the second urgent request of Lucetta for her letters to Henchard, and the reading of those letters to Lucetta's husband by Henchard, who finds them in the safe of his old home, now Farfrae's. It will be remembered from

the discussion of incident eight that Henchard's attempt
to return the letters was unsuccessful both in the serial
and in the book, but that in the one they remained in
the hands of Farfrae, to whom they had been entrusted
by Elizabeth Jane, and in the other in the hands of
Henchard. Accordingly, upon the second request for
her letters, which Lucetta makes of Henchard in Casterbridge market, his reply to her in the book must
needs differ from his reply to her in the serial. In the
former, after a surprised exclamation intended to
throw the blame upon her failure to receive the letters
on the day of her intended stop in Casterbridge while
en route to Budmouth, he promises to consider what
he did with the parcel, and later recollects that he left
it in his old safe.[13] In the latter, a far longer conversation is necessary in view of Henchard's own ignorance as to the whereabouts of the letters, as well as for
a portrayal of Lucetta's natural anxiety and of Henchard's natural curiosity:

"I have returned the whole lot of your letters."

"I think not," she said timidly.

"I tell ye I returned every scrap of your handwriting —
returned 'em long ago!"

"Then I never received them."

"I sent them to you in a packet by Elizabeth Jane, and she
put them into your hands when you were passing through Casterbridge by coach — exactly as you requested."

"Ah, I did not take that journey till some days later."

"Then what did Elizabeth Jane do with them?" said he.
"You had better find out."

Lucetta's anxiety was now to see Elizabeth Jane, which there was not much difficulty in doing. She called by request, and then Lucetta learned how Farfrae, as may be remembered, had offered to deliver the packet to relieve Elizabeth from the tedium of waiting at the coach-office.

What had become of those letters, Lucetta asked herself, after they had passed so strangely into Donald's hands? Why had they never left his possession, when that possession was to have been but the trusteeship of a moment? She could only hope that the packet had been destroyed.

And yet it was of the essence of Farfrae's careful nature never to destroy anything.

.   .   .   .

Henchard's thoughts were running on a parallel line with those of poor Lucetta's.

.   .   .   .

As soon as his work was over, he, too, went to Elizabeth Jane, to make the inquiry in which Lucetta had preceded him. To him also Elizabeth confessed that she had been relieved of the parcel by Farfrae.[14]

The reading of the letters to Farfrae by Henchard on the evening following Lucetta's request for them differs in serial and book only in the necessary changes in wording, evidenced in the treatment of the interview between Henchard and Lucetta in incident fourteen. As in the discussion of that incident, these differences are best shown by quoting from the Harper edition, the corresponding parts from the serial being placed in brackets :*

* Note again that the portions italicized occur only in the book, and *not* in the serial, that the serial material is in brackets, and that the rest is common to both.

"For me," Henchard read [the letter went on], "there is practically no future. *A creature too unconventionally devoted to you* [A wife whose husband has vanished into thin air] who feels it [morally] impossible that she can be wife of any other man; [after going to the altar with you;] and who is yet no more *to you* [your wife] than the first woman you meet in the street — *such am I* . . . that in the event of your present wife's death you will *place* [restore] me *in her position* [to my true position] is a consolation so far as it goes — but how far does it go? Thus I sit here, *forsaken by my few acquaintance, and forsaken by you!* [a widow without the melancholy satisfaction of a husband's tomb.]" [15]

If the demand for sensationalism on the part of the readers of the *Graphic* is evident in Lucetta's saving of the life of Henchard, in the meeting of Mrs. Henchard and Lucetta, and in the much-heightened bull episode, it is even more apparent in the treatment of incident eighteen, in which Lucetta meets Henchard by appointment and secures from him a promise of the letters. Her letter to him, in which she asks him to meet her at the Ring[16] is practically identical in serial and book,[17] but there are most interesting differences in her preparation for the meeting. So well, indeed, do these differences illustrate the apparent contrast in viewpoint between the reader of periodical fiction and the novel reader of the late Victorian era that I think it worth while to quote both the passages descriptive of her preparation.

From the Harper edition:

To herself she said, on closing up this appeal: "If ever tears and pleadings have served the weak to fight the strong, let them do so now!"

With this view she made a toilette which differed from all she had ever attempted before. To heighten her natural attractions had hitherto been the unvarying endeavor of her adult life, and one in which she was no novice. But now she neglected this, and even proceeded to impair the natural presentation. She had not slept all the previous night, and this had produced upon her naturally pretty though slightly worn features the aspect of a countenance ageing prematurely from extreme sorrow. She selected — as much from want of spirit as design — her poorest, plainest, and longest discarded attire.[18]

From the serial:

To herself she said, on closing up this appeal: "If ever tears, artifice, hypocrisy, have served the weak to fight the strong, let them do so now!"

With this view she spent the whole afternoon in making a toilette which differed from all she had ever attempted before. To heighten her natural attractions had hitherto been the unvarying endeavor of her adult life, and one in which she was no novice. But now she systematically proceeded to impair the natural presentation. In two hours she had produced upon her naturally pretty though slightly worn features the aspect of a countenance withering, ageing, sickly — a head of hair with a few incipient grey threads; in brief, prematurely wrecked by extreme sorrow.

The chemist up the street, who eked out a meager drug trade by scented soaps, cosmetics, and disfiguring ointments of various kinds, was three or four times requisitioned for this proceeding. By the time she had sicklied herself to her mind the hour had arrived.

It was with a shudder, almost with a terror, that she beheld in the glass what she had done. It seemed too real. If her dear husband should meet her he would surely believe that this was her true aspect, and that her hitherto charming lineaments had been the counterfeit of art.[19]

Nor is the sensational in the serial version limited to Lucetta's preparation for the meeting. There, after the account of the meeting, which does not differ significantly from that in the book,[20] the author adds another complete episode to the chapter — an episode dealing with the unexpected meeting with Farfrae, who comes to seek Henchard on business. It will be remembered that in the novel Farfrae, on the day preceding the eventful reading of the letters by Henchard, proposes to the town-clerk that they place Henchard in a small seed-business, but is deterred by the clerk's information that Henchard is Farfrae's bitter enemy.[20] So also in the serial. The change of mind on Farfrae's part and his determination to place Henchard in the business whether or no are given only in the following serial episode, obviously to motivate Farfrae's seeking for Henchard, and thus to afford a splendid chance for a bit of melodrama, dear to the heart of the magazine reader:

The evening had closed into night, and their remaining words were few. Respect, affinity of ideas, genial comradeship — the only permanent bases of affection between other than blood relations — had never entered into Henchard's sentiments toward Lucetta, and now that her freshness and elasticity seemed to have departed, he experienced no passion for or against her.

A head and shoulders suddenly broke above the western summit of the amphitheatre, rising higher by degrees. Some idler had, for once, apparently chosen to ramble there. "Hist!" said Henchard. Lucetta pulled down her veil.

. . . .

Before his wife came out that evening, Farfrae had, without entering the house, gone from the corn-stores into the town on a business which he had once before begun and abandoned. Henchard's visit had awakened a slight chord of feeling for him, by reason of their past friendship, and he resolved that, after all, he would do what he could toward purchasing the seed-business for the fallen man. He went up the street, and having money in his purse, soon contrived to set the affair again in train. This done, he was anxious to let Henchard know of it early, and went on to his cottage. Here he learned from Jopp that Henchard had gone out by the Budmouth Road. Farfrae followed, but saw no Henchard. Confronted by the amphitheatre, eloquent at silent evening-time, he mounted the earthworks where Lucetta and Henchard saw him at once against the sky, though he could not see them in the gloom of the vast concavity. Farfrae walked round on the summit, and descended the slope by the great entrance just as Henchard and Lucetta passed through it to come out. A meeting could not be avoided, and Henchard conducted himself boldly as was his wont.

"Ah — it is Henchard, I think?" said Donald.

"Yes," said Henchard.

"I have been looking for you — I have some news to tell ye. But no — I won't interrupt you now," Farfrae said, his eyes for the first time falling on the female figure.

"It don't matter," replied Henchard quietly, perceiving that Donald had no suspicion as to the personality of his companion, owing to the unusual wrappings she wore. "Is the news serious?"

"'Tis good news," said Farfrae cheerfully. "News I'm right glad to have to tell ye, man. About the seed-business, you know. We shall be able to arrange it for ye after all."

They had walked on together, through the gloom, Henchard drawing Lucetta's arm through his own to lend a delusive aspect to the rendezvous he had been surprised in, and keeping her on the outside. Farfrae proceeded to state the details of the proposal, which he did without reserve, being under the impression that if, as it seemed, Henchard were about to contract another marriage, he could have no secrets from his future partner. "Well, and will ye accept?" he asked.

Henchard, feeling how deeply he had wronged Farfrae in suspecting him of enmity to the scheme, could not reply at once. And certain pride kept him from jumping at the offer. He thanked Donald for his exertions on his behalf, said he would think the matter over; adding, "I have still strong arms, you know, and can keep myself without assistance as far as that goes."

"And will add another to yourself soon apparently," said Farfrae playfully, nodding to Henchard's companion. Henchard made no answer to this; and feeling himself one too many in such circumstances, Farfrae bade them Good-night and went his way.

Lucetta and Henchard parted immediately Donald left them, Lucetta passionately longing to get back to her husband, whose bearing toward Henchard had so moved her during her enforced silence as almost to lead her to fling her arms round his neck, regardless of consequences. She crept indoors like a shade, and ascended to her room. When she had restored herself to her natural hues, she went down and found her husband in the dining room.

"Well, Lucetta, I've a bit of news for ye," he said gaily, "I think poor Henchard is going to console himself by speculating in a wife once more. I met him courting just now."

In the treatment of incident twenty-four, which is the subject of chapters xlii and xliii of both serial and book,* there are interesting and most significant changes in the plot. In the book Henchard, out one day on the Budmouth Road to see if, by means of his telescope, he can spy Farfrae and Elizabeth Jane at their courting, sees from the rampart of an old fort a masculine figure coming along the road from Budmouth. By means of the telescope Henchard discovers that the man is Richard Newson. No other alternative is left him, in the face of past events, but to leave Casterbridge. He goes that same evening at dusk, Elizabeth Jane accompanying him a short distance and parting from him "with unfeigned wonder and sorrow." But her wonder, as well as her sorrow, leave her when an hour later she finds her own father, Newson, awaiting her at Donald Farfrae's. In place of such emotions she can have only joy over her father's return, and resentment at Henchard's treatment of her and of her father.

Now, in the serial version of the story, events are handled very differently. The incident of Henchard's discovery of Newson on the Budmouth Road and of his subsequent decision to leave Casterbridge is entirely omitted in the serial.[21] To be sure, he decides to leave, but that decision is satisfactorily motivated, not by the

* The chapters are numbered the same in both serial and book.

appearance of Newson but by the love affair of Farfrae and Elizabeth Jane. As to Newson, we learn in
the serial story, though not until the close of the chapters in question, that his existence in Budmouth is
known for some weeks, even months, by Elizabeth
Jane, that her walks two or three times a week on the
Budmouth Road (which in the book are to afford her a
glimpse of the sea) are for the purpose of meeting him,
and that she with Donald Farfrae knows of his intended arrival at Farfrae's house. To be sure, her
mysterious walks in the direction of Budmouth are
sufficient, and, obviously, designed to arouse the interest and curiosity of the magazine reader, but such
suspense is gained by a sacrifice of plausibility, and,
therefore, of art. For could a reader be found, even
a periodical reader of the eighties, so credulous as to
accept without question the situation of a girl who, having learned of the existence of her own father and
meeting him often, still continues to live in peace and
affection with a stepfather who has grossly deceived
her, and parts from him with "unfeigned regret"? [22]

In discussing the last and most important incident —
the return of Henchard to Elizabeth Jane's wedding,
her reproof of him, and his departure — it is necessary
to recall the author's statement in the preface of the
Osgood-M'Ilvaine edition in 1895: "The present edition of the volume contains *nearly a chapter* which has
never yet appeared in any English copy, though it was
printed in the serial issue of the tale, and in the American edition."

From this statement it is evident that this additional "chapter" is common alike to both serial version and Harper edition. A comparison of the two versions of it (chapter xliv) shows few differences and those insignificant. Obviously the dissimilarity is to be found between the earlier English editions in which the chapter "has never yet appeared" and our Harper standard edition, which in 1895 bore the imprint of Osgood, M'Ilvaine and Company, and which, in this case, as I have said, is practically identical with the serial.

The difference is perfectly apparent when one compares chapter xliv in either the serial or the Harper edition with the corresponding chapter of the first (English) edition, that of Smith, Elder and Company, London (1886).[28] And so important is it that the discussion cannot, in this instance, be consigned to a note, a consignment which I announced in the preface would be my procedure with reference to first editions. In the first edition, chapter xxi of volume two is meager, indeed not more than a third as long as the corresponding chapter in the serial and in the Harper edition — and it omits an important circumstance and a more important incident. It will be remembered that in our familiar edition Henchard, upon his departure from Elizabeth Jane, returns "at length" to his old work of hay-trussing. This is true also in the serial. But in the first edition, though he starts out equipped with his tools, he is pictured as seeking no employment but only wandering about, from Weydon Priors back toward Casterbridge, "surveying mankind" and meditating meanwhile upon the cruel inconsistencies of life. And, what is more important, the chapter does not contain the story of Henchard's return to Elizabeth Jane's wedding, the culminating tragedy of both serial and Harper editions.[24] In the first edition we know of the wedding only as it might have been seen by Henchard, "had he been able to extend his vision through the night shades as far as Casterbridge." I quote the passage which affords that description:

Had he been able to extend his vision through the night shades as far as Casterbridge that evening, Henchard would have seen that the door of his old house was wide open, that the hall was lighted extravagantly, and that people were going up and down the stairs. It was the wedding day of Elizabeth and Farfrae. Such an innovation on Casterbridge customs as a flitting of bride and bridegroom from the town immediately after the ceremony had not been thought of, and at that hour Mr. and Mrs. Farfrae were entertaining a houseful of guests at their home in Corn Street.

Donald himself was taking a leading part in the festivity, his voice being distinctly audible in the street, giving expression to a song of his native country. Idlers were standing on the pavement in front, and presently it could be perceived that a dance was proposed, Mr. and Mrs. Farfrae joining in the figure.

Then the people without could discern fractional parts of the dancers whenever their gyrations brought them near the windows, together with about two-fifths of the band in profile, including the restless shadow of a fiddler's elbow and the tip of the bass-viol bow. With the progress of the dance the performers spread out somewhat, and Elizabeth was distinctly visible.

She was in a dress of white silk or satin — the observers were not near enough to say which — snowy white without a tinge of milk or cream; and the expression of her face was one of nervous pleasure rather than gaiety. Presently Farfrae came round, his exuberant movement making him conspicuous in a moment. The pair were not dancing together this time, but it was apparent that there was a wordless speech between them; and that whenever the interchanges of the figure made them the partners of a moment their emotions breathed a much subtler essence than at other times.

By degrees the idlers became aware that the measure was also trod by someone who out-Farfraed Farfrae in saltatory intenseness. This was strange, and it was stranger to find that the eclipsing personage was Elizabeth Jane's partner.

The first time they saw him, he was sweeping grandly round, his head quivering and low down, his legs in the form of an X, and his back towards the door. The next time he came round in the other direction, his white waistcoat preceding his face, and his toes preceding his white waistcoat. That happy form was Captain Newson's.[25]

With this passage the chapter under discussion comes to a close in the first edition. The final chapter of the story, which deals with Mr. and Mrs. Farfrae's discovery of the death of Henchard, alone save for Abel Whittle (chapter xlv in the serial and the Harper edition; chapter xxii, vol. II, in the first edition), does not in its several versions show many more dissimilarities than obviously necessary. With the exception of some improvements in diction made in the Harper edition, and of a few other minor changes, the chapter in the book is almost identical with that in the serial. As to the first edition there are differences which are, of course, necessary in view of the preceding chapter. Obviously Elizabeth Jane's determination to seek her stepfather cannot be motivated, as it is in the serial and in the Harper edition, by her discovery of the dead goldfinch. It is rather brought about by the recurring thought of her stepfather, most natural since she is living in his old home. Except for these differences, however, the last chapter of the novel varies little in any edition examined.[26]

After noting carefully the differing conclusion of the story in the early English editions as compared with that of both serial and Harper editions, one will certainly agree with "the good judges across the Atlantic, who strongly represented that the home edition suffered from the omission" of Henchard's return to the wedding, of his pathetic gift to his daughter, and of his more pathetic departure. It is difficult, indeed, to understand what line of reasoning could have decided the author to take this incident from the serial version when he was revising the serial for publication in book form. It must have been that, in his effort to avoid the sensational and the melodramatic in his finished product, he so far misinterpreted the effect of Henchard's return upon his readers as to sacrifice, in the early English editions, the culminating episode which so fittingly brings his great tragedy to a close.

CHANGES IN CHARACTERIZATION

It is best, I think, before proceeding with this division of my comparison, to define the term "characterization" as I shall use it here. In presenting the changes made in the delineation of character from serial to book, I shall consider here only, first, those made by the author in his description or analysis of the character; and second, those suggested by the characters themselves in conversational passages common to both serial and book. To illustrate: I do not consider the obvious difference in Lucetta's character between the serial and the book upon the occasion when she prepares herself to meet Henchard in the Ring a definite change in characterization, for the simple reason that the different treatment of the incident *calls for* a different Lucetta. On the other hand, the several differing statements in regard to Elizabeth Jane's personality in passages common to both serial and book unquestionably suggest a desire on the part of the author to present a different conception of her character; that is, here he is not *compelled* to change her to make her consistent with the action in question.

With this explanation in mind I shall now show the major differences between the serial and the book versions of the story in the delineation of certain characters, notably those of Elizabeth Jane and Farfrae.

Henchard, the dominant character, differs not at all in serial and book. Because of the addition of a long story which he tells in the serial version at the public dinner in Casterbridge, and which is entirely lacking in the book,[27] the magazine reader might have gathered that he was more loquacious than he is represented in the later version, though that impression was surely not strengthened by other similar additions, and, indeed, seems out of place in the serial. Lucetta, too, is practically the same person in both serial and book. In the former she is slightly younger than in the latter, and "handsome" in the one while merely "pretty" in the other.[28] In the serial she is the daughter of a merchant, while in the book her father is an army officer, to which fact she attributes her tendency to be "flighty and unsettled."[29] But except for these minor details, the author has evidently no wish to make the characters of either Henchard or Lucetta distinctly different in the book from what they were in the serial.

With the characterization of Elizabeth Jane and Farfrae, however, the case is certainly different. As to the former, Hardy had unmistakably a different conception of her in the revision of the serial; as to the latter, if the author's conception of him was not different in the book, it was, to say the least, more clear.

A difference in the characterization of Elizabeth Jane is suggested in the very beginning of the story, where Hardy takes the trouble to change the color of her eyes. They are blue in the serial; in the book they are black.[30] One somehow instinctively feels that this change in color is suggestive of two different young women. The blue-eyed Elizabeth Jane of the serial is characterized by such adjectives as "sensible" and "unselfish,"[31] "simple" and "sober"; her black-eyed counterpart of the book is never described as sensible and unselfish, she is "studious" instead of "simple,"[32] and "quiet" instead of "sober."[33] She of the serial is,

moreover, not particularly pleasing to look upon — at
least we are told of no attractiveness; we read, however, of the "budding beauty" [34] and "peachy cheeks" [35]
of her of the book, and are informed that she "could
now have been writ handsome." [36] In the serial she is
"ignorant" [37] and "uninstructed"; [38] in the book, only
"unfinished" and "unsophisticated." According to
the serial: "Knowledge, learning, accomplishments;
those, also, she had not"; [39] according to the book:
"Knowledge — the result of great natural insight —
she did not lack; learning, accomplishments — those,
also, she had not." [40] Both Elizabeth Janes study, but,
whereas the one in the serial is content with "a copy-
book, and a dictionary and a grammar of my native
tongue," [41] the other buys herself "grammar-books and
dictionaries and a history of all the philosophies." [42]
"She began the study of Latin, incited by the Roman
characteristics of the town she lived in." [43] Her lapses
in speech became "really slight . . . for she read
omnivorously." [44] She of the serial is possessed of a
simple piety which expresses itself in such words as
these uttered when safety from the attack of the bull is
assured: "Thank God, 'tis all right now. He always
protects us when we don't expect Him to." [45] She of
the book, on the contrary, is characterized as "subtle-
souled." [46] Surely these changes in adjectives from
serial to book, these additional sentences in the book
descriptive of Elizabeth Jane's studies, were not made
without a definite purpose on the part of the author of

transforming a rather colorless, unintelligent girl, into an attractive, well-informed, ambitious, and sensitive young woman, who by her greater individuality adds immeasurably to the interest of the story.

It is very apparent to one who compares in the various versions of *The Mayor of Casterbridge*[47] the passages relating to Donald Farfrae, and most especially the conversation of that Scotchman, that Hardy's conception of him as a true representative of his native land, if it did not change, at least constantly became clearer and more consistent.   The most significant changes in his dialect occur in the revision of the serial for the first edition.   Here there are eighteen distinct changes,[48] either in spelling or in phraseology, to suggest a more pronounced Scotch accent.   But a comparison of the first and second editions, in which Farfrae's language is identical, with that of the standard Harper (a reprint of the Osgood, M'Ilvaine and Company edition of 1895), shows also most interesting alterations made in preparation for this edition of 1895.   The preface to the 1895 edition, given in the standard Harper, suggests an explanation of those changes.   I quote from the preface:

"It must be remembered that the Scotchman of the tale is represented not as he would appear to other Scotchmen, but as he would appear to people of other regions.   Moreover, no attempt is made herein to reproduce his entire pronunciation phonetically, any more than that of the Wessex speakers.   I should add, however, that this new edition of the book has had the accidental advantage of a critical overlooking by a professor of the tongue in question — one of undoubted authority: — in fact he is a gentleman who adopted it for urgent personal reasons in the first year of his existence."

The "professor of the tongue in question" apparently suggested the seven distinct changes[49] from first and second editions to the later one. It seems as unnecessary to quote these changes as to attempt to catalogue those eighteen evidenced in the comparison of the serial with the book. One will serve as an example.

In the serial issue of the story and in the first and second editions, Farfrae says to Henchard:

"Come, you know better than all this, sir. It is tyrannical and unworthy of you."

In the later edition the passage is emended to read:

"Come, a man o' your position should ken better, sir! It is tyrannical and no worthy of you." [50]

This illustration is typical of the other alterations in Farfrae's dialect, the inclusion of which is forbidden because of lack of space.

Aside from his dialect Farfrae has no distinctively Scotch traits which are emphasized in the serial version of the tale, or, indeed, in the first edition of the story in book form. But at some time during the few months or a year between the first and the second edition, Hardy must have decided to attach to the second character of his novel some characteristics decidedly Scotch, at least from the Englishman's viewpoint; for in the second edition (Sampson Low, 1887) we find two changes in phraseology which differ from the corresponding diction of both the serial and the first edition, but which are identical with those in the Harper edition. The first change occurs when Henchard is criticising Farfrae's entertainment held in celebration of a certain national event. He says in the serial version of the story, "Charge admission at so much a head!" and in the first edition, "Charge admission at so much a head — just like him!" But in the second and in the Harper editions, Hardy grows bolder, and makes Henchard say, "Charge admission at so much a head — just like a Scotchman!" [51]

The second change occurs in the last chapter of the story where Farfrae and Elizabeth Jane search for Henchard. Farfrae, deliberating over the advisability of camping for the night says, in the second edition and in the Harper, with the thriftiness popularly attributed to his countrymen, "And that will make a hole in a sovereign." [52] He does not, however, make any such remark in the serial or in the first edition. Finally, in the Harper edition, in the chapter descriptive of Henchard's return to the wedding, Farfrae is described as "giving strong expression to a song of his dear native country, *that he loved so well as never to have revisited it.*" [53] Since this chapter is lacking from the first and the second editions, the passage is, of course, also lacking. In the serial version the italicized portion with its obvious satire is omitted, very probably for reasons of the editor's own.

CHANGES IN SETTING

In a discussion of the changes in setting apparent in the several versions of *The Mayor of Casterbridge*, one fact must be kept well in mind: In 1895 Osgood, M'Ilvaine and Company of London published the first volume of the so-called Wessex Novels edition; in 1897 the imprint changed to that of Harper and Brothers.[54] The proposed title of the new edition without question instigated certain changes in the setting of at least some of the novels,[55] the aim of the author quite obviously being to heighten the Wessex atmosphere of the stories, first, by more definitely featuring the geography; and second, by making the speech of his Wessex characters, especially of his rustics, more dialectic. In each of the new novels was printed, presumably for the first time in any edition, a map of Wessex.[56]

A statement of the author in the preface to the new edition of *The Mayor of Casterbridge*, which preface is also used in the Harper edition, suggests, I think, his first intention in regard to heightening the Wessex atmosphere in this novel:

"Some shorter passages and *names*, omitted or altered for reasons which no longer exist, in the original printing of both English and American editions, have also been replaced or inserted for the first time."

It is, of course, impossible to assure oneself of the "reasons, which no longer exist," for the original omissions or alterations. It is not unlikely, however, that, like many authors featuring a certain locality, Hardy felt a natural reticence, especially in the earlier versions of his stories, toward too definitely revealing the setting of his novels.

The use of the word Wessex itself in the several versions of *The Mayor of Casterbridge* forms an interesting bit of investigation.   In the very beginning of the story in the first and second editions the location of Weydon-Priors "in Upper Wessex" is omitted, though the phrase occurs in the serial and in the Harper edition.   Again, at the close of chapter ii the location of Casterbridge "in a far distant part of Wessex" is omitted from the serial and from the first and second editions, though it is given in the Harper edition.   But even more interesting than the presence or absence of the word Wessex is the very definite increase of geographical names in the Harper edition.   The author's intention is clearly to pay more heed to setting — in other words, to make his locality stand out more clearly.   As soon as the novels begin to bear the name Wessex Novels, as soon as *The Mayor of Casterbridge* becomes distinctly a Wessex story, "a river" in the serial and earliest book editions becomes "the river Froom," [57] known to Hardy readers through the tragic honeymoon of Tess and Angel Clare; "a hill" becomes "Yalbury Hill," [58] the very one, we remember, of the familiar versions of *Under The Greenwood Tree* and *Far from the Madding Crowd*.   The "White Hart Vale" of the serial and earliest book editions does not ring familiarly in our ears as does "The Vale of Blackmoor" [59] to which it is changed in the Harper edition, and which has been forever immortalized to Hardy readers by *Tess*. The names of towns, many of which are absent in the serial and the first and second editions, add materially to the Wessex atmosphere and suggest other stories in which they also occur: Shottsford,[60] the town in which Henchard purchased the goldfinch for Elizabeth Jane, is mentioned also in *Tess of the D'Urbervilles*, in *Jude the Obscure*, in *Far from the Madding Crowd*, and in *The Woodlanders*; Weatherbury,[61] mentioned as one of the places visited by Henchard in his wanderings after the wedding, recalls memories of Fanny Robin and the child in *Far from the Madding Crowd* and of Gabriel Oak and Bathsheba; Anglebury,[62] one of the localities referred to in the search for Henchard, is reminiscent of *The Return of the Native*; Kingsbere,[63] which is Stickleford in the serial and first and second editions, is inevitably suggestive of the D'Urberville knights and ladies in their coffins.

It would, indeed, be interesting to discover to what extent Hardy in his serials and in the first editions of his other earlier novels omitted or altered these Wessex names, which are so familiar to his readers of the later editions. That, however, must form the basis for another piece of investigation. Suffice it to say that, in *The Mayor of Casterbridge* at least, the Wessex atmosphere is unmistakably stressed and strengthened in our present version of the story, and that this stressing and strengthening was without doubt made before the so-called Wessex edition was published.

And now what of the second means of heightening
the Wessex atmosphere — the change in the speech of
the Wessex characters, especially of the Wessex rustics?
There are some thirty passages in the Harper edition
which show a distinct alteration of corresponding passages, common in this matter to serial and to first and
second editions.   Hardy was most evidently anxious
that the Wessex edition of *The Mayor of Casterbridge*
should be more true in Wessex atmosphere than the
previous editions.   I shall not take time to summarize
these changes.[64]   Many of them occur in the alteration
of the pronoun "you" to "ee," "him" to "en," and of
the verbs "are" or "get" to "be," and "saw" to "zeed,"
and by far the greater number of them are in the conversation of the Wessex rustics.   Two quotations — the
first, an excerpt from the discussion among the rustics
of Christopher Coney's theft of the pennies on the dead
Mrs. Henchard's eyelids; and the second, the gossip of
the rustics concerning Farfrae and Lucetta on the occasion of the Royal Personage's visit — will serve to
illustrate these alterations.   I place in brackets the
words common to the serial and to the first and second
editions.

First passage:

"Well, and Martha did it, and buried the ounce pennies in
the garden.   But if ye'll believe words, that man, Christopher
Coney, went and dug 'em up and spent 'em at the Three Mariners [King o' Prussia].   'Faith,' he said, 'why should death rob
life o' [of] fourpence?   Death's not of such good report that
we should respect 'en [honour him] to that extent,' says he."

"'Twas a cannibal deed!" [nevertheless] deprecated her listeners, [shaking their heads].

"Gad, then, I won't quite ha'e it," said Solomon Longways. . . . I wouldn't speak wrongfully for a zilver zixpence [silver sixpence] at such a time. I don't see *noo* (omitted in serial and first and second editions) harm in it. . . . Money is scarce, and throats be [get] dry. Why should death rob [deprive] life o' [of] fourpence?" [65]

Second passage:

In the crowd stood Coney, Buzzford, and Longways. "Some difference between him now and when he zang [sang] at the Dree Mariners [King o' Prussia]," said the first.

"'Tis wonderful how he could get a lady of her quality to go snacks wi'en [with him] in such quick time."

"True. . . . Now there's a better-looking woman than she that nobody notices at all, because she's akin to that hontish [manly] fellow Henchard."

· · · · · · · · · · ·

"That's not a noble passiont [passion] for a 'oman [woman] to keep up," said Longways.[66]

Slight as these changes are in themselves, the number of passages in which they occur certainly serves to show that Hardy made a conscious effort to emphasize the distinctly Wessex dialect of his characters.

Certain Minor Additions and Alterations

It seems best to present under this general head the addition of several passages to the book version of *The Mayor of Casterbridge* — passages entirely lacking in the serial form of the story, though present in the first and succeeding book editions. They were very evidently added for the sake of giving a more literary atmosphere to the novel — an atmosphere probably not demanded and perhaps not appreciated by many serial readers. Few though they are (there are six) they unmistakably add literary tone. I quote them with the necessary context, in each case italicizing the added portions. The portions not italicized are common to both serial and book:

(1) The Amphitheatre was a huge circular enclosure, with a notch at opposite extremities of its diameter north and south. *From its sloping internal form it might have been called the spittoon of the Jötuns.*[67]

(2) Everybody was attracted, and some said that her (Elizabeth Jane's) bygone simplicity was the art that conceals art; *the "delicate imposition" of Rochefoucauld*; she had produced an effect, a contrast, and it had been done on purpose.[68]

(3) The landscape over the river disappeared; *the wind played on the tent-cords in Aeolian improvisations*; and at length (the wind) rose to such a pitch that the whole erection slanted to the ground, those who had taken shelter within it having to crawl out on their hands and knees.[69]

(4) Henchard *felt like Saul at his reception by Samuel; he* remained in silence for a few moments, then throwing off the disguise of frigidity which he had hitherto preserved, he said, . . .[70]

(5) In the latter quarter of each year cattle were at once the mainstay and the terror of families about Casterbridge and its neighborhood, *where breeding was carried on with Abrahamic success.*[71]

(6) The proceedings had been brief — too brief — to Lucetta, *whom an intoxicating Weltlust had fairly mastered*; but they had brought her a great triumph nevertheless.[72]

Under this same heading, also, I am mentioning some other very minor changes from serial to book, which, in spite of their unimportance, do, in my opinion at least, add to the atmosphere of the novel. These are changes obviously made for the sake of emphasizing color, and I believe they deserve some little space. Henchard's house, which is "fronted with murrey-colored old brick" in the serial, is in the book faced with *"red-and-grey"*;[73] the iron railings are "painted a bright *green*" instead of the "chocolate" of the serial.[74] The "ermined" judge of the Casterbridge court becomes a *"red-robed"* one in the book,[75] and the "surfaces of hedged fields" become "square *green* areas."[76]

Slight as these changes seem, do they not add vividness and concreteness to the whole, and do they not suggest an interesting appreciation of detail on the part of the author?

CHANGES IN DICTION

It seems unfortunate that the many changes in diction apparent upon a study of the several versions of *The Mayor of Casterbridge*, and in themselves significant enough to form the basis of no mean investigation, should perforce be relegated to so small a subdivision of the study as this must be. These alterations, with very few exceptions, occur in the revision of the serial for book publication — that is, they are present in the first as well as in the Harper edition.

Most of these changes in diction are evidenced by the substitution of a single word for another less specific or for a phrase still less exact, though there are other alterations obviously made for the purpose of keeping a figure. Of these word substitutions there are one hundred and seventy-five. It seems injudicious to quote even the page references for such a number, and impossible to give examples of more than a few of the most interesting:

(1) In the first chapter, together with several other changes in diction, Michael Henchard's *implement* in the serial becomes a *hoe* in the book.[77]

(2) In the same chapter the *points* of his character are changed to *qualities*.[78]

(3) The furmity-woman of the fair knows, in the serial, "the taste of the *thoughtless* females"; in the book, "of the *shameless* females." [79]

(4) In the serial Elizabeth Jane discovers in her mother's speech an indication of her failing health by her *"finality of tone"*; in the book, by her *"renunciatory tone."*[80]

(5) In the serial the pathos of Donald's song, by an intruding noise, was temporarily *displaced*; in the book, temporarily *effaced*.[81]

(6) Henchard's remarriage to his wife is known in the serial as a *reinstallation*; in the book as a *reinstation*.[82]

(7) At Elizabeth's news that she is to leave her father, he responds, according to the serial in this way: " 'Where?' said Henchard, *his facial activities suspended."* According to the book: " 'Where?' said Henchard, *his face stilling."* [83]

These examples serve to show Hardy's method in the improvement of his diction.[84] The quotation of two sentences will, I think, illustrate his care in the matter of figures, apparent in his revision of the serial.

(1) From the serial: "He, Henchard, would sink to the position of second fiddle, and *be only a spectator* of his manager's talents."

From the book: "He, Henchard, would sink to the position of second fiddle, and *only scrape harmonies* to his manager's talents." [85]

(2) From the serial: "As a maxim glibly repeated from childhood remains practically unmarked till some mature experience enforces it, so did this High *Street* Hall now for the first time really show itself to Elizabeth Jane, *though her eyes had glanced over it* on a hundred occasions."

From the book: "As a maxim glibly repeated from childhood remains practically unmarked till some mature experience enforces it, so did this High *Place* Hall now for the first time really show itself to Elizabeth Jane, *though her ears had heard its name* on a hundred occasions." [86]

NOTES

[1] See pages 90 to 96 in Harper edition.

[2] *Ibid.*, pp. 93-94.

[3] *Graphic*, vol. 33, p. 134.

[4] *Ibid.*, p. 135.

[5] The chapters in serial and book are numbered the same. It is impossible to give in detail all minor passages which show changes, eliminations, or additions. These are shown in the annotated volume of *The Mayor of Casterbridge* presented to the library of the University of Minnesota.

[6] See note 8.

[7] *Graphic*, vol. 33, p. 135.

[8] See pp. 139-144 in Harper edition.

[9] These changes from serial to book may be seen in the annotated *Mayor of Casterbridge*, p. 140, in the University of Minnesota library.

[10] *Graphic*, vol. 33, p. 217.

[11] From pp. 235-236 in Harper edition.

[12] See pp. 246-248 in the Harper edition, and p. 342 in the *Graphic*, vol. 33, or the annotated book, which gives both versions of the episode.

[13] See pp. 293-294 in Harper edition.

[14] *Graphic*, vol. 33, p. 398.

[15] From p. 296 in Harper edition.

[16] An ancient amphitheatre in Casterbridge.

[17] See p. 300 in Harper edition.

[18] *Ibid.*, p. 301.

[19] *Graphic*, vol. 33, p. 422.

[20] See pp. 289-290 in Harper edition.

[21] See pp. 375, 376, 377, in Harper edition.

[22] It may seem strange that, with changes so significant from serial to book as these in incident twenty-six, no passages from the serial are given. The lack of them is explained by the statement that the changes in the book are brought about through the addition of passages rather than through the omission of those in the serial. There are many minor alterations and omissions, but none which lend themselves to quotation.

[23] The first edition is in two volumes. The chapter in question is chapter xxi, vol. II.

[24] If one is interested to know the exact length and almost identical material of the chapter in the first edition, he may discover both by reading chapter xliv in the Harper edition, beginning p. 385, as far as p. 387, paragraph beginning, "At length he obtained employment," and by then adding the material of the passage given from the first edition.

[25] See p. 297, vol. II, Smith, Elder & Company edition (1886).

[26] In the second edition, that published in 1887 by Sampson Low, Marston, Searle & Rivington, the last two chapters are identical with those of the first edition.

[27] See p. 69 in *Graphic*, vol. 33, or page 41 in the annotated book.

[28] See p. 179 in Harper edition, the annotated copy if possible.

[29] See p. 180 in Harper edition.

[30] *Ibid.*, p. 7.

[31] See p. 154 in annotated book (Harper edition).

[32] *Ibid.*, p. 167.

[33] *Ibid.*, p. 394.

[34] *Ibid.*, p. 114.

35 *Ibid.*, p. 158.

36 *Ibid.*, p. 160.

37 *Ibid.*, p. 115.

38 *Ibid.*, p. 104.

39 *Ibid.*, p. 104 or p. 162 in the *Graphic*, vol. 33.

40 See p. 104 in Harper edition (the annotated preferred).

41 See p. 115 in annotated book.

42 *Ibid.*, p. 115.

43 *Ibid.*, p. 158.

44 *Ibid.*, p. 155.

45 See p. 249 in annotated book, or p. 342 in the *Graphic*, vol. 33.

46 See p. 142 in Harper edition (the annotated preferred).

47 The serial version, the first edition (Smith, Elder & Co., 1886), the second edition (Sampson Low, Marston, Searle & Rivington, 1887), and the standard Harper.

48 These may be found on the following pages of the Harper edition: 54, 57, 77, 93, 112, 118, 131, 132, 188, 190, 193, 194, 204, 205, 290, 328, 329, 382; and can be compared with the corresponding expressions in the serial by the use of the annotated book.

49 I give the page references in the first edition (identical in this matter with the second) together with the corresponding references in the Harper editions. The seven changes may be found as follows: Smith, Elder & Co. ed., vol. I, p. 90 and Harper ed., p. 58; S. E., vol. I, p. 119 and H. p. 76; S. E., vol. I, p. 188 and H. p. 119; S. E., vol. I, p. 191 and H. 121; S. E., vol. I, p. 196 and H. 123; S. E., vol. II, p. 8 and H. p. 202; S. E., vol. II, p. 154 and H. p. 296.

50 The first form of the quotation is found on p. 188, Smith, Elder & Co. edition, vol. I; the second on p. 119, Harper edition.

51 For serial and Harper version, see annotated book, p. 123; for version in the first edition, see Smith, Elder & Co. edition, vol. I, p. 196; for version in the second edition, see Sampson Low edition, p. 141.

52 See Sampson Low edition, p. 427, and Harper edition, p. 402.

53 See p. 393, Harper edition.

54 There is every reason to think that the Harper edition is identical with that of 1895. There is, in fact, almost positive assurance that this is true in the case of *The Mayor of Casterbridge*. *The Mayor* was one of three novels not out of print at the time of the transfer to Harper and Brothers, who took over the stock of novels on hand and

rebound them in Harper's cloth.   (See A. P. Webb, *A Bibliography of the Works of Thomas Hardy*, p. 74.)   It is extremely unlikely that any changes would have been made after such a procedure.

[55] I have already shown in my Master's thesis the evidence of those changes in *The Well-Beloved*, and I shall later show it in the case of *Tess of the D'Urbervilles*.

[56] See the collations of the editions in A. P. Webb, *A Bibliography of the Works of Thomas Hardy*.

[57] See p. 197, Smith, Elder & Co., vol. I, or p. 124 of annotated Harper edition in the University of Minnesota library.

[58] See p. 392 in annotated Harper edition.

[59] *Ibid.*, p. 117.

[60] Shottsford does not occur in serial, first, or second editions.   See p. 390 in Harper edition.

[61] Weatherbury does not occur in serial, first, or second editions. See p. 401 in Harper edition.

[62] See p. 40 in Harper edition.   Anglebury does not occur in serial, first, or second edition.

[63] See p. 72 in annotated Harper edition.

[64] Anyone interested in exactly the situations in which these changes occur may consult pp. 4, 19, 35, 95, 101, 143, 144, 147, 148, 235, 293, 300, 302, 322, 328, 329, 336, 347, 351, 352, 374, 378, 389, 399, 403 — preferably in the annotated Harper edition.

[65] See pp. 143-144 in annotated Harper edition referred to above.

[66] *Ibid.*, p. 322.

[67] See p. 84 in Harper edition.

[68] *Ibid.*, p. 115.

[69] *Ibid.*, p. 125.

[70] *Ibid.*, p. 223.

[71] *Ibid.*, p. 246.

[72] *Ibid.*, p. 325.

[73] *Ibid.*, p. 74.

[74] *Ibid.*, p. 103.

[75] *Ibid.*, p. 109.

[76] *Ibid.*, p. 225.

[77] *Ibid.*, p. 3.

[78] *Ibid.*, p. 7.

[79] *Ibid.*, p. 25.

[80] *Ibid.*, p. 30.

[81] *Ibid.*, p. 61.

[82] *Ibid.*, p. 153.

[83] *Ibid.*, p. 174.

[84] There are relatively few changes in diction between the first and the Harper editions. There is one, however, so good that it deserves mention, both for itself and for the reason that it shows Hardy as constantly improving his choice of words. In the first and second editions as well as in the serial, Henchard and his wife emanate in the first chapter "an atmosphere of *domesticity*"; in the Harper edition it becomes one of *"stale familiarity."*

[85] See Harper edition, p. 166.

[86] *Ibid.*, p. 166.

TESS OF THE D'URBERVILLES

TESS OF THE D'URBERVILLES

IF we accept Mr. Hardy's statement in the explanatory note to the first edition of *Tess of the D'Urbervilles* (Osgood, M'Ilvaine and Company, London, 1891), we shall not need to question whether the serial form of the story is earlier than the book form. He says:

"The main portion of the following story appeared — with slight modifications — in the *Graphic* newspaper; other chapters, more especially addressed to adult readers, in the *Fortnightly Review* and the *National Observer*, as episodic sketches. My thanks are tendered to the editors and proprietors for enabling me now to piece the trunk and limbs of the novel together, and print it complete, as originally written two years ago."

From this statement we are to infer that the first form of *Tess of the D'Urbervilles* was written in 1889; that this version is the one published as the first edition in 1891; and that the serial form of the story, published in the *Graphic*, July 4, to December 26, 1891, is a revision of the first form, modified apparently to meet the demands of editor and public.

It is not easy, however, for one who has carefully compared the serial version with those of the first and later editions to accept Mr. Hardy's statement, at least

in its entirety.   Without doubt the form of the story
familiar to us all in the present standard Harper edition — which is, in its main outlines, identical with the
first edition of 1891 — was, as he says, the *first* form
of the story, as far as incident and plot are concerned.
When he revised that form for serial publication, he
made rather more than "slight modifications" in incident and plot, having in mind, as I have said, the
demands of the *Graphic* editor and the taste of the
Graphic readers.   But most certainly (and here is
where I must question his statement) he did *not* make
good sentences into bad ones, or substitute inexact
words for specific ones.   Nor did he exclude purposely
from his serial version certain literary references designed to give tone to his novel.   By such evidences as
these I have, therefore, reached my conclusion as to
the exactness of the statement in the preface, and
postulate the following assumption:

The first form of the novel was, in incident and plot,
the story as we know it today, but in the essentials of
style it was inferior.   When the author prepared it for
serial publication, he omitted certain incidents and
altered others, probably at the request of the editor, so
as not to offend the taste of the magazine readers.   He
did not, however, improve the sentence structure or the
diction, nor did he strengthen the literary atmosphere.
These improvements were made later, after some
experimentation, most of them, to be sure, occurring in
the revision from serial to first edition (as in the case

of *The Mayor of Casterbridge*), but not a few being made in the revision of one edition for another. The chapter which follows will, I am sure, prove the validity of this assumption.

CHANGES IN INCIDENT AND PLOT

Following the method of procedure in the corresponding chapter on *The Mayor of Casterbridge*, I shall first of all summarize the main incidents of the plot of *Tess of the D'Urbervilles*, starring those most significant to this study. I am again assuming that the reader is familiar with at least the main outlines of the present standard version of the story, upon which version my summary is based.

The incidents which form the plot are as follows:

1. John Durbeyfield, higgler, of the village of Marlott, is informed by Parson Tringham, an antiquarian, that he is the lineal representative of the knightly family of the D'Urbervilles, and, obsessed with the new idea, grows more shiftless than ever.

2. His daughter Tess, who feels herself responsible for the death of their one horse, consents against her will to seek assistance, through employment if possible, from the D'Urbervilles of Trantridge, the family of a tradesman who has taken the name for social prestige.

3. Tess goes to Trantridge, meets Alec D'Urberville, and is, a week later, offered the position of manager of his mother's poultry, presumably by that lady herself.

4. With a good many misgivings she accepts the offer and goes to Trantridge, where she is thrown into closer association with Alec D'Urberville.

*5. At the close of a Saturday evening in Chaseborough, a neighboring town, D'Urberville rescues Tess from her companions, who have been drinking, takes her out of the main road under pretense of getting her safely away, and seduces her in the woods of The Chase.

*6. After a few more weeks at Trantridge Tess starts homeward, and meets on the way a painter of scriptural texts.

*7. Upon reaching home, she tells her mother her story.

*8. Her child is born, is taken ill some weeks later, is baptized by Tess herself, and is refused Christian burial by the vicar.

*9. Two years later Tess goes to Talbothays Dairy as a dairymaid.

10. At Talbothays she meets Angel Clare, who is the son of the Vicar of Emminster, and who is studying practical dairying.

11. They fall in love and Clare presses Tess to marry him, but she decides she cannot on account of her past.

*12. Three milkmaids at the dairy, who are also in love with Clare, are carried across a pool of water in his arms on a certain Sunday morning.

13. Tess, unable to resist her love for Clare, prom-

ises to marry him, and is advised by her mother to tell him nothing of her past.

14. A few days before her marriage, however, she writes a letter to Clare, confessing all, but on her wedding morning finds it, still undiscovered by him, under the carpet in his room where it slipped in her hurried placing it beneath his door.

15. They are married and go on their honeymoon to a farmhouse near Wellbridge, once the manor-house of a D'Urberville.

16. Here Tess, having listened to Angel's confession of dissipation with a strange woman, tells the story of her own past, and is repulsed by her husband.

17. Angel walks in his sleep, carries Tess in his arms over the Froom bridge and into the Abbey grounds, and is induced by her to return home, he all the while completely unconscious.

18. They decide to separate for a time, she to return home, and he to go to Emminster and from there, perhaps to South America.

*19. Returning to the Wellbridge house to pay the rent for their stay, Clare meets Izz Huett and asks her to go to Brazil with him. Izz accepts, but Clare comes to himself and leaves her.

20. Eight months later Tess, having heard nothing from Clare, goes to Flintcomb-Ash to work with Marian (one of the Talbothays dairymaids) in the turnip fields.

21. Tess discovers Alec D'Urberville, who has been converted by Angel Clare's father, preaching in a barn.

22. He follows her, insists on renewing their acquaintance in spite of her remonstrance, comes to see her at Flintcomb-Ash, and finally, through passion for her, gives up his new-found religion.

*23. Tormented by his advances, Tess writes to Angel telling him of her exposure to temptation and begging him to come to her or to send for her, and the letter, having reached Emminster Vicarage, is sent on to Brazil.

*24. Clare in Brazil begins to question his attitude toward Tess, confides in a stranger who tells him he was wrong in his treatment of her, and finally, having received Tess's letter from Flintcomb-Ash, determines to go home to her at once.

25. Tess, hearing that her mother is ill, returns to Marlott to assume family responsibility, to bury her father, and to be still pestered by Alec D'Urberville.

*26. Completely discouraged, and frightened at D'Urberville's persistence, she writes Angel Clare upbraiding him for cruelty.

*27. The Durbeyfields, having lost the lease of their cottage, move to Kingsbere, are deprived of their lodgings, and camp near the tombs of their ancestors, from which situation they are taken by Alec D'Urberville to Trantridge.

*28. Angel Clare returns home, finds Tess's upbraiding letter, hesitates to confront her suddenly, and writes her mother, from whom he receives an unsatisfactory reply.

29. A letter from Izz Huett and Marian determines him to go at once in search of Tess.

*30. He finds her at Sandbourne living with Alec D'Urberville, whom she, upon Clare's departure, stabs to death.

31. She follows Clare, and they, after journeying through the woods all day, live for five days in a deserted manor-house before continuing their journey to eventual discovery at Stonehenge.

32. Tess is tried for murder and hanged at Wintoncester.

And now to the presentation of the differences existing between the starred incidents of the book and the corresponding incidents of the serial.

The first significant difference between the book and the serial in the treatment of an incident, and hence in the development of the plot, occurs in incident five — by all means the most important incident of the novel, since upon it hangs nothing less than the story itself. This all-important episode is the seduction of Tess by Alec D'Urberville in the woods of The Chase near Trantridge. Its details are familiar to all readers of Hardy — the Saturday night revels in Chaseborough, Tess's walk homeward with certain none too steady companions, the quarrel that ensues between her and Car, the Queen of Spades, D'Urberville's sudden arrival and rescue of her, their ride through The Chase with its culminating tragedy.[1] The announcement that almost none of this material is in the serial may come as a surprise, but it is nevertheless true. Chapters x and xi are entirely lacking in the magazine version of the story, with the exception of the following sentences which are placed in the serial at the close of the preceding chapter:[2]

But where was Tess's guardian angel now? Perhaps, like the god of whom the ironical Tishbite spoke, he was talking, or he was pursuing, or he was on a journey, or peradventure he was sleeping and was not to be awaked. As Tess's own people down in those retreats are never tired of saying among each other, in their fatalistic way, "It was to be." There lay the pity of it.[3]

These chapters were, however, published as an "episodic sketch" in a Special Literary Supplement of the *National Observer* for November 14, 1891, under the title of "Saturday Night in Arcady," [4] but the connection between this sketch and the *Graphic* serial running at the same time was presumably not made apparent.[5] The readers of the serial, then, were deprived, probably by the judgment of an astute editor rather than by the decision of Hardy himself, of the motivating incident of the story, and instead were obliged to be satisfied with Tess's rehearsal to her mother of Alec D'Urberville's deception, as she gives it in the serial treatment of incident seven, which treatment I shall soon present.

In the treatment of incident six — the departure of Tess from the D'Urberville estate and her ironical encounter on the way homeward with the painter of scriptural texts — there is another significant omission

from the serial version. The narrative of her departure, of Alec's overtaking her, and of their conversation has few changes, and those only the necessary ones
in view of the fact that, since the seduction is omitted
in the serial, all references to it must be likewise omitted
or altered. But an important change occurs in the
omission from the serial of the entire episode of the
meeting with the painter of texts. It will be remembered that after D'Urberville has left her, Tess is
approached by and drawn into conversation with the
text-painter, who carries her basket for her, and who
stops now and again to paint a text on a stile or a con-
venient wall: "Thy, Damnation, Slumbereth, Not,"
and "Thou, Shalt, Not, Commit ———." The serial
contains no such episode, obviously because, since it
omits the seduction of Tess, it would be inconsistent in
portraying the "accusatory horror" [6] engendered in her
by the sight of the texts. Moreover, the editor of the
Graphic, if we may draw conclusions from other similar omissions from the same serial story, may have considered it politic at least to keep from his magazine in
the early nineties a sentence such as this: "Some people
might have cried, 'Alas, poor Theology!' at the hide-
ous defacement — the last grotesque phase of a creed
which had served mankind well in its time." [7]

Thus far, as we have seen, the serial version of our
novel has no motivating incident for Tess's departure
from Trantridge other than the suggestions given in
the passage recently quoted in the discussion of incident
five,[8] and in her conversation with Alec D'Urberville

on the way homeward. We get that necessary motivating incident in the serial from Tess's rehearsal of her story to her mother. The differences between book and serial in the treatment of that rehearsal are so significant that I think it well to quote each in its entirety. The conversation between Joan Durbeyfield and her daughter is as follows.

From the book:

"Well! — my dear Tess!" exclaimed her surprised mother, jumping up and kissing the girl. "How be ye? I didn't see you till you was in upon me! Have you come home to be married?"

"No, I have not come for that, mother."

"Then for a holiday?"

"Yes — for a holiday; for a long holiday," said Tess.

"What! isn't your cousin going to do the handsome thing?"

"He's not my cousin, and he's not going to marry me.'

Her mother eyed her narrowly.

"Come, you have not told me all," she said.

Then Tess went up to her mother, put her face upon Joan's neck, and told.

"And yet th'st not got him to marry 'ee!" reiterated her mother. "Any woman would have done it but you!"

"Perhaps any woman would except me."

"It would have been something like a story to come back with, if you had!" continued Mrs. Durbeyfield, ready to burst into tears of vexation. "After all the talk about you and him which has reached us here, who would have expected it to end like this? Why didn't ye think of doing some good for your family instead o' thinking only of yourself? See how I've got to teave and slave, and your poor weak father with his heart clogged like a dripping-pan. I did hope for something to come out o' this! To see what a pretty pair you and he made that day when you drove away together four months ago! See what he has given us — all, as we thought, because we were his kin. But if he's not, it must have been done because of his love for 'ee. And yet you've not got him to marry!"

Get Alec D'Urberville in the mind to marry her! He marry *her*! On matrimony he had never once said a word. And what if he had? How she might have been impelled to answer him by a convulsive snatching at social salvation she could not say. But her poor foolish mother little knew her present feeling towards this man. Perhaps it was unusual in the circumstances, unnatural, unaccountable; but there it was; and this, as she had said, was what made her detest herself. She had never cared for him, she did not care for him now. She had dreaded him, winced before him, *succumbed to a cruel advantage he took of her helplessness; then, temporarily blinded by his flash manners, had been stirred to confused surrender awhile; had suddenly despised and disliked him, and had run away.*[9] That was all. Hate him she did not quite; but he was dust and ashes to her, and even for her name's sake she scarcely wished to marry him.

"You ought to have been more careful, if you didn't mean to get him to make you his wife!"

"O mother, my mother!" cried the agonized girl, turning passionately upon her parent as if her poor heart would break. "How could I be expected to know? I was a child when I left this house four months ago. Why didn't you tell me there was danger in men-folk? Why didn't you warn me? Ladies know what to fend hands against, because they read novels that tell them of these tricks; but I never had the chance o' learning in that way, and you did not help me!"

Her mother was subdued.

"I thought if I spoke of his fond feelings and what they might lead to, you would be hontish wi' him and lose your chance," she murmured, wiping her eyes with her apron. "Well, we must make the best of it, I suppose. 'Tis nater, after all, and what do please God." [10]

From the serial:

"Well! — my dear Tess!" exclaimed her surprised mother, jumping up and kissing the girl. "How be ye? I didn't see you till you was in upon me! Have you come home to be married?"

"No, I have not come for that, mother."

"Then for a holiday?"

"Yes — for a holiday; for a long holiday," said Tess.

Her mother eyed her narrowly. "Come, you have not told me all," she said.

Then Tess told.

"He made love to me, as you said he would do, and he asked me to marry him, also just as you declared he would. I never have liked him, but at last I agreed, knowing you'd be angry if I didn't. He said it must be private, even from you, on account of his mother; and by special license, and foolish I agreed to that likewise, to get rid of his pestering. I drove with him to Melchester, and there in a private room I went through the form of marriage with him as before a registrar. A few weeks after, I found out that it was not the registrar's house we had gone to, as I had supposed, but the house of a friend of his, who had played the part of the registrar. I then came away from Trantridge instantly though he wished me to stay; and here I am."

"But he can be prosecuted for this," said Joan.

"O, no — say nothing!" answered Tess. "It will do me more harm than leaving it alone."

Joan thought so too, "as it was all in their own family," and silence was accordingly determined on and kept. Moreover, she could not help asking herself if it might not be a legal marriage after all? Stranger things had been known.[11]

The most cursory comparison of these two passages will establish certain outstanding facts. First, there is an obvious difference in the motivating incident of the novel: In the book Tess is seduced by Alec; in the serial her virtual seduction is made more palatable by the fact that she *thought* she was marrying him, though the marriage was in reality a sham. Second, there is a lack of motivation for the marriage itself: Tess marries Alec to escape her mother's anger and to "get rid of his pestering," two very insufficient reasons, it seems to me, and not easily credible in view of the character of Tess as delineated up to this point in the story. Third, there is a decided difference in the character of Tess as she is depicted in the two accounts: In the book she has been "temporarily blinded by his flash manners, . . . stirred to confused surrender awhile; had suddenly despised and disliked him, and had run away."[12] In the serial she comes away from Trantridge the instant she knows of the deceit practiced upon her. Fourth, there is perfectly evident literary superiority in the account in the book over that in the serial: Tess's recital in the serial is not only lacking in dramatic force, but it is unnatural in the extreme. She does not speak like an indignant and heartbroken girl, who has been grossly deceived, but rather in the constrained artificial tones of one who has learned her speech by rote. Joan, too, in the serial is certainly not her excitable, superficial, easily-swerved self. She shows not the slightest emotion over her daughter's story, merely stating in words unlike her own, and with a perspicacity quite foreign to her, "But he can be prosecuted for this."

Finally, in view of the preceding facts, I assume that the serial version of incident seven is a makeshift, substituted in place of the book version, unwillingly, no doubt, and, I must think, without sufficient care by Hardy, who must have known that it lacked in itself sufficient motivation, consistency of character, and literary merit, but who was constrained either by his editor or by his own judgment to refrain from shocking the conventionalized taste of the *Graphic's* reading public.

The discussion of incident eight — the birth of Tess's child, its illness, her baptism of it, and its burial [13] — requires but little space here, for the simple reason that its details are entirely lacking from the serial version of the story. The Tess of the serial has no child. Indeed, her one wrongdoing, which is solely responsible for the awful weight of ensuing tragedy, is the sham marriage with D'Urberville. One questions why, with the marriage established, Hardy should have felt it necessary to omit from the serial the birth of the child with the succeeding events of its illness, baptism, and burial. Tess was, according to the serial, in complete ignorance of the invalidity of the marriage for some weeks. Why then should the birth of a child be a disgrace? And it would so greatly add to the sum total of mishaps, because of which Angel Clare was later to repulse her. In other words, it would help to strengthen the motivation of the novel, which is, in the serial, so deplorably weak. For, what reason can Angel Clare have for repudiating a girl who has married a man in good faith and left him the moment she finds that the marriage is false? The taste of those *Graphic* readers must have been overly squeamish — more dictatorial, indeed, than their appreciation of art; for this dramatic episode in the story was not allowed space, either by an editor who knew his public or by an author who could not afford to offend.

The episode was published, however, in the *Fortnightly Review* for May, 1891, a few weeks before the *Graphic* serial began, under the title "The Midnight Baptism: A Study in Christianity." A comparison of it with the corresponding material in chapter xiv of the book reveals no significant differences. The *Fortnightly* sketch is abridged, the interest being centered on the single character, and the description of the field which figures in the book version being omitted. There is no apparent connection between it and the novel, since Tess is never known by her own name, but is called "the girl in pink," "the pink girl," or "Sis." The past tense is used throughout, instead of giving way to the present as in the book.

The question as to why the *Fortnightly Review* could publish with impunity material which the *Graphic* must needs decline is a question which I am reserving for later consideration.

The treatment of incident nine — the journey of Tess two years later to Talbothays Dairy — varies from the serial to book version in but one particular, and that is in her visit to the church at Kingsbere, wherein lay the bones of her knightly ancestors. This incident is common to both versions, to be sure, but in the book it does not take place until near the close of the story, when the Durbeyfields, deprived of their Kingsbere lodgings, determine to camp by the wall of the church.[14] In the serial, however, Tess makes her pilgrimage to the tombs of her fathers on her way to Talbothays. The account is as follows:

Tess had never before visited this part of the country, and yet she felt akin to the landscape. Not so very far to the left of her she could discern a dark patch in the scenery, which inquiry confirmed her in supposing to be trees, marking the environs of Kingsbere — in the church of which parish the bones of her ancestors — her useless ancestors — lay entombed.

She had no admiration for them; not a single material thing of all that had been theirs did she retain but the old seal and spoon; yet to diverge from the direct route in order to glance at their resting-place was a passing courtesy to which they were entitled, and no serious task for so active a walker. Tess entered the church about two in the afternoon, and beheld for the first time in her life the spot whereof her father had spoken or sung with painfulness ever since Parson Tringham's announcement.

Here stood the tombs of the D'Urbervilles — formed of grey Purbeck marble; canopied, altar-shaped, and plain; their carvings defaced and broken; their brasses torn from the matrices. Of all the reminders that she had ever received that they were socially an extinct family there was none so forcible as this spoliation.

She drew near to a dark stone, on which was inscribed:

Ostium sepulchri antiquae familiae D'Urberville.

Tess did not read Church-Latin like a Cardinal, but she knew that this was the door of her ancestral sepulchre, and that the tall knights of whom her father chanted in his cups lay inside it in their leaden shrouds.

"Pooh, what's the good of thinking about them!" she said with a sudden sigh. "I have as much of mother as father in me — all my prettiness comes from her, and she was only a dairymaid." [15]

It must be granted that the position of the incident in the book is far more advantageous from a dramatic point of view than this placing of it in the serial; but since I shall have further occasion to deal with the episode itself, as well as with its position in the story, I shall not here comment at greater length upon it.

There is an interesting, if not significant, change from serial to book in the handling of incident twelve — the episode of Angel Clare's assistance to Tess and to the three other milkmaids, Marian, Izz, and Retty, on a certain Sunday morning. The situation will be remembered. The four girls start in their best clothes for church, but their progress is checked by a pool of water in the lane, the result of a bad storm the night before. Angel arrives upon the scene and offers to carry them across, which offer makes each girl tense with emotional excitement. He takes each in his arms in turn — Marian, Izz, and Retty — and carries her safely to the other side. Then he returns for Tess, whispering as she lowers herself into his arms, "Three Leahs to get one Rachel." [16]

The alteration in the serial version is almost absurd. Here instead of carrying the girls across in his arms Clare goes to a neighboring shed and procures a wheelbarrow in which he wheels each in turn across the pool.[17] It is hardly necessary to observe that a scene which is idyllic in the book becomes almost burlesque in the serial. The alteration is, to be sure, insignificant in its bearing on the plot of the story, but it forms an interesting example of the sacrifice of the æsthetic to the conventional!

Another sacrifice for the sake of propriety is evident in the serial treatment of incident nineteen — Clare's return to the Wellbridge house and his invitation to Izz Huett, whom he meets there and who confesses her love for him, to accompany him to Brazil. A comparison of their conversation, which I am quoting first from the book and then from the serial, speaks for itself and needs no further comment.

From the book:

"I am going to Brazil alone, Izz," said he. "I have separated from my wife for personal, not voyaging, reasons. I may never live with her again. *I may not be able to love you*,[18] but will you go with me instead of her?"

"Do you truly wish me to go?"

"I do. I have been badly used enough to wish for relief. And you at least love me disinterestedly."

"Yes — I will go," said Izz, after a pause.

"You will? You know what it means, Izz?"

"It means that I shall *live*[19] with you for the time you are over there — that's good enough for me."

"Remember, you are not to trust me in morals now. But I ought to remind you that it will be wrong-doing in the eyes of civilization — Western civilization, that is to say."

"I don't mind that; no woman do when it comes to agony-point, and there's no other way."

"Then don't get down, but sit where you are."

He drove past the cross-roads, one mile, two miles, without showing any signs of affection.[20]

From the serial:

"I am going to Brazil alone, Izz," said he. "I have separated from my wife for personal, not voyaging, reasons. So keep me company a little while longer."

"I don't mind," said she.

"Then don't get down, but sit where you are."

He drove past the cross-roads, one mile, two miles, without showing any signs of affection, and the conversation was continued on the subject of Brazil, Clare asking her jestingly if she would like to go with him. Concerned to find from her affirmative that she took the question seriously, he said no more on that matter, and they lapsed into silence.[21]

Incidents twenty-three, twenty-four, twenty-six, and twenty-eight, all of which deal with the letters from Tess to Angel Clare, are, I think, best discussed together, in their relations to the corresponding portions of the serial. Tess's first letter to Angel is written at Flintcomb-Ash, on the evening of the day when Alec D'Urberville has come to the wheat-field to force his attentions upon her again. The letter in the book is identical with that in the serial,[22] but there is a difference in the matter of its receipt by Angel in Brazil. In the book the letter is sent on directly to him from Emminster Vicarage:

"Now," said old Mr. Clare to his wife, when he had read the envelope, "if Angel proposes leaving Rio for a visit home at the end of next month, as he told us that he hoped to do, I think this may hasten his plans, for I believe it to be from his wife." He breathed deeply at the thought of her, and the letter was redirected, to be promptly sent on to Angel.[23]

In the serial, however, Mr. Clare determines to keep the letter, believing that Angel is leaving for home too soon to receive it before he sails:

"Now," said old Mr. Clare to his wife, when he had read the envelope, "if Angel proposes leaving Rio for a visit home at the end of *this* month, as he suggested to us that he would do, I must not send any more letters on to him, or he and they will cross in mid-ocean." [24]

There is, consequently, a difference between book and serial in the reception of the letter by Angel. In the former he receives it and decides to hasten homeward, a decision which has been formulating in his mind during the weeks in Brazil — weeks of regret for his "hasty judgment" [25] of her and of "growing fondness for her memory";[26] in the latter he does not receive it at all, since his parents keep it at the vicarage until they hear that he has postponed his sailing, upon which announcement they forward it to him, but too late for him to receive it.

But though in the serial he receives no letter from her, he writes to her, his letter dictated by his regret, by his shame, and by his realization of her goodness and purity:

In recalling her face again and again, he thought now that he could see therein a flash of the dignity which must have graced her grand-dames; and the vision sent that *aura* through his veins which he had formerly felt; and which left behind it a sense of sickness.

It resulted in his writing her a passionate letter, declaring that he forgave her all, and would return in a few weeks. But that letter she never received. Using the direction of Flint-comb-Ash that she had given him, he addressed her in her married name, which her reticence had never allowed her to assume; and when, in the course of a month, the missive reached the post-office of that village, it was promptly returned to the head-office as being that of a person unknown. The result was less to be deplored in that he was unable to return as soon as he had stated, but the assurance might have for the moment cheered, though it would afterwards have disappointed, her.

Meanwhile Tess's warm outpouring lay awaiting him in a drawer at Emminster Vicarage, its ardour pitifully wasting itself on the cold darkness and impercipience of that receptacle, like a star whose rays reach no inhabited planet. The writer, with an enlarging conviction that Angel would come soon in response to the entreaty, addressed her mind to the tender question of what she could do to please him best when he should arrive.[27]

In the book he does not write her, trusting to his arrival to set things right once more.

Meanwhile, in the book version, Tess writes him again on the eve of Old Lady-Day, the date of their enforced relinquishment of the cottage and of their moving to Kingsbere, and after another attempt of Alec D'Urberville to force himself upon her. Alec has come to see her at Marlott during the absence of her mother and the children, has taunted her and sneered at her "nice husband," and has insisted that, instead of going to Kingsbere, they move to his cottage at Trantridge. Tess, stung to desperation by D'Urberville's insistence and for the moment overcome by her sense of the injustice she has suffered at the hands of Angel, writes him a second letter.

She passionately seized the first piece of paper that came to hand, and scribbled the following lines:

"O, why have you treated me so monstrously, Angel! I do not deserve it. I have thought it all over carefully, and I can never, never forgive you! You know I did not intend to wrong you — why have you so wronged me? You are cruel, cruel, indeed! I will try to forget you. It is all injustice I have received at your hands! — T." [28]

In the serial no such letter is written, though her desperation and her sense of the injustice she has suffered are described practically as they are in the book.

And now as to Angel's return home, his receipt of the second letter, and his hesitation to go at once to Tess.

His hesitation is, in the book, obviously incited by the receipt of Tess's upbraiding letter, which makes him doubtful of her love and of the wisdom of his plan to go at once in search of her. He thinks it will be best to write first to her mother, announcing his return and inquiring the whereabouts of Tess. Joan Durbeyfield's reply, and her promise to inform him when Tess shall return home, delay him still longer. Finally a warning letter from Marian and Izz Huett, beginning: "Honor'd Sir, — Look to your Wife if you do love her as much as she do love you," and signed, "From Two Well-Wishers," [29] sends him on his way.

In the serial, on the other hand, his hesitation is motivated by the facts, first, that he has received no reply to his letter to her sent to Flintcomb-Ash and never claimed; and second, that he has never received her letter from Flintcomb-Ash, which his father kept to await his return and then sent on too late for its reception by him. He therefore waits at Emminster for a fortnight, until the letter shall come back. With this letter is the one from Marian and Izz, both of which start him at once on his way.

It is perhaps useless to comment on these differing motives for delay. Neither, it must be admitted, seems adequate in the face of such a situation. His hesitation in the serial, however, is almost more excusable, inasmuch as he is ignorant of her appeal to him in her letter from Flintcomb-Ash, and as he does not know that she has not received his letter addressed to her there. In the book, I think, he has less excuse. He has received her appeal, and it seems hardly plausible that the justly upbraiding tone of her second letter should prevent him from going to her at once.

This more excusable delay in the serial may, indeed, have appealed to Hardy as an opportunity to mitigate somewhat the selfishness and short-sightedness of Angel Clare, and also to make an appeal to the serial reader by the pathos of his fortnight of waiting for the letters to come back, and also by the tears that blind his eyes when, immediately upon the receipt of her appealing letter, he springs "up wildly to go to her." [30] On the other hand, the book version is rendered more dramatic and more consistent by her writing of the second letter, instigated, as was the first, by the ominous persistence of Alec D'Urberville.

To return now to the treatment of incident twenty-seven — in which the Durbeyfield family, deprived of their Kingsbere lodgings, camp near the tombs of their ancestors. It will be remembered that, just as they with their goods and chattels are nearing Kingsbere, they are met by a man who informs them that their lodgings have been let. Tess is desperate at this intelligence, but her mother, after a moment of anxiety, decides to unload their belongings near the church, insisting that one's family vault is his own freehold. She accordingly sets up the bed by the church wall, puts the younger children in it, and starts toward the town. On the way she meets Alec D'Urberville, who asks for Tess, and who, upon finding that she is near or in the church, goes there himself. Tess meanwhile enters the

Kingsbere church for the first time in her life, and gazes upon the tombs of her ancestors. As she gazes, the sight of a recumbent figure upon a slab makes her start as she thinks she has seen it move. It proves to be Alec D'Urberville, who has appeared at a critical moment, when, at least in Mrs. Durbeyfield's opinion, they have no alternative but to accept his offer of a lodging.

It will be obvious to one who knows the story at all that this incident is really the climax of the plot, for because of it Tess, now desperate, returns to Alec D'Urberville and thereby seals the fate of him, of Clare, and of herself. It will be evident also that the incident in itself adds tense dramatic force to the story. Moreover, the irony suggested by the visit of Tess to the ancient D'Urberville sepulcher after all she has endured is a hundred fold more poignant here than in the serial, where, as I have explained in the treatment of incident nine, her visit takes place on her way to Talbothays.

Now, in the serial story there is nothing of this material. The family move to be sure, but to Shottsford-Forum instead of to Kingsbere, and are met by the man with the information as to their lodgings, but here the incident closes, with these words:

The man went his way, and the defenceless family turned to each other to join in a council of war; for hostilities seemed to environ them on every side.[31]

It is difficult to see why Hardy should have excluded from his serial story an episode of such dramatic, even sensational, appeal.　Surely by it the taste of no reader could have been offended, and his interest would most certainly have been enhanced.　One is tempted to surmise that even in the original form of the story this incident may have been lacking.　May not Hardy have added it in the general renovation under which that original form most surely went before its publication as the first edition?

The last incident which shows significant differences between its treatment in the book and in the serial is Angel Clare's discovery of Tess at The Herons in Sandbourne, where she is living with Alec D'Urberville.　The details are practically identical in both accounts, but there are slight alterations in the serial version, which are important because of the suggestion they give as to the relations existing between Alec D'Urberville and Tess.　For example, upon Angel's inquiry at the door for Teresa D'Urberville, the landlady asks, in the serial, "Miss D'Urberville?"; whereas in the book she says, "Mrs. D'Urberville?" [32]　The difference clearly suggests that the serial reader was by no means to suppose that Tess lived with Alec as his wife.　Again, the conversation between Tess and Angel is, in the serial, by alterations and omissions intended to convey the same impression.　The quotation of corresponding passages will illustrate this.

From the book:

"I waited and waited for you!" she went on, her tones suddenly resuming their old fluty pathos.　"But you did not come, and I wrote to you, and you did not come!   .   .   .   He was very kind to me, and mother, and to all of us after father's death. He —"

"I don't understand."

"He has won me — back to him."

Clare looked at her keenly, then, gathering her meaning, flagged like one plague-stricken, and his glance sank; . . .

She continued: "He is upstairs   .   .   .   I hate him now, because he told me a lie — that you would not come again; and you have come. *These clothes are what he has put upon me; I didn't care what he did wi' me.*[33] But will you go away. Angel, please, and never come any more!" [34]

From the serial:

"I waited and waited for you!" she went on, her tones suddenly resuming their old fluty pathos. "But you did not come, and I wrote to you, and you did not come!   .   .   .   He was very kind to me, and mother, and to all of us after father's death. He —"

"I don't understand."

"He has won me — to be friends with him."

Clare looked at her keenly, then, gathering her meaning, flagged like one plague-stricken, and his glance sank; . . .

She continued: "I hate him because he told me a lie — that you would not come again. But — will you go away, Angel, please, and never come any more!" [35]

The same intention on the part of the author to give a different impression in the serial as to the relations between Tess and Alec — to gild them with a moral tinge — is evidenced in chapter lvi, the chapter following Angel's departure from Tess. We are told in the

book that Mrs. Brooks' best apartments at The Herons
have been taken by the week by the "D'Urbervilles";
in the serial, "for Miss D'Urberville by a cousin of the
latter." [36]   Again, although in the book Tess upbraids
Alec in her desperation, in the serial she speaks *of* him,
never *to* him, the inference of course being that they
do not share the same apartment.   In fact, in the serial
Tess crosses to "another apartment," which, we are
told, is "sometimes occupied by her cousin, Mr. D'Urberville," [37] and there stabs him.

It is surely unnecessary to comment upon the fact
that these serial alterations are almost absurd, and
must surely have tested the credulity of any reader possessed of average intelligence.   If Tess is living in
another apartment from Alec, if he has won her simply
"to be friends with him," why the tragedy when she is
face to face with Angel?   Again, if the reader of the
serial is to believe that Tess and Alec are not living
together as man and wife, how then is he to reconcile
the revengeful murder of Alec?   Would it not have
been better, since the *Graphic* editor was so insistent
upon conventional relations, for Hardy to have legitim-
ized the sham marriage with which he so poorly motivated his serial story in the beginning?   That situation
would at least have given some excuse for the events
that follow.   Surely, one cannot believe that even a
reader of magazine fiction of the Victorian era could
have been so gullible as to accept without question these
glaring absurdities!

CHANGES IN CHARACTERIZATION

Unlike *The Mayor of Casterbridge, Tess of the D'Urbervilles* presents few changes in characterization from book to serial (or from serial to book, as the case may well have been with the minor differences). In fact, if we eliminate, as of course we must, the necessary alterations in character suggested by the different treatment of an incident, and limit the changes, as we did in *The Mayor of Casterbridge*, first, to those made by the author in the description or analysis of a character; and second, to those suggested by the characters themselves in conversational passages common to both serial and book, we find almost no differences in characterization apparent between book and serial. There are, however, a few slight alterations which I am mentioning, but which, I think, are not particularly significant, interesting though they may be.

Twice in the book a difference occurs in Hardy's treatment of Tess. These changes were, I think, made in the renovation of the first form of the story, before it was published in the first edition rather than in the preparation for serial publication, because they are more consistent with the character of Tess in the present version of the story.

In Hardy's description of her in the serial, as she appears in the "club-walking" at the beginning of the story, she is "a fine handsome girl — not handsomer than some others, certainly, — but her soft peony cheeks and large innocent eyes added eloquence to

color and shape." [38]   In the book he substitutes her
"mobile peony mouth" for her "soft peony cheeks."
Not only is the change to be preferred on the score
that a mouth naturally is more eloquent than cheeks,
but also that it suggests to one familiar with the story
the frequent mention of Tess's mouth, which exerts a
fascination over both Alec D'Urberville and Angel
Clare.   This alteration in the beginning, therefore,
makes for greater consistency.

Again, Hardy characterizes in the serial the nature
of Tess as "impulsive and tender."   In the book he
calls it "large and impulsive." [39]   The substitution of
"large" for "tender" is certainly far more consistent
with the impression he wishes to give of her in the
book.

The other difference in characterization occurs in the
dramatic scene at Wellbridge farmhouse in which
Tess confesses her past to Angel, and it suggests a
slightly different conception of Clare.   Because of
three alterations in that scene, Angel is made to appear
even less sympathetic in the serial than he is in the
Harper edition.   First, he speaks to Tess "coldly," [40]
as he does not do in the familiar book version; indeed,
there he speaks "tremulously," [41] which he does not do
in the serial.   Second, when she tells him of her plan
to kill herself with the cord of her box, he says in the
serial, "If you do not want to sink still lower in my
esteem, you will promise me to attempt that no more"; [42]
in the book, however, he is less harsh toward her: "You
must not dare to think of such a horrible thing.   How

could you! You will promise me as your husband to attempt that no more." Finally, in the serial Tess speaks to Angel as "sir," and as "Mr. Clare," — forms of address which would certainly imply greater coldness, even cruelty, on his part.[43]

With the exception of these very minor alterations, however, I can find no evidences on Hardy's part of a different conception of his characters in the various versions of *Tess* which I have examined and compared.

Changes in Setting

In my treatment of the changes in setting from earlier to later editions of *The Mayor of Casterbridge*, I attempted to show that these changes were made in preparation for the publication of the Wessex Novels edition in 1895, basing my evidence, first, on the more definite featuring of Wessex geography in the edition of 1895, and second, on the more distinctly Wessex dialect of the characters. In the presentation of changes which help to emphasize the Wessex setting in *Tess of the D'Urbervilles*, I shall base my evidence wholly on the dialectic changes, since there are no significant geographical alterations or additions.[44]

The changes in dialect are, however, interesting, and I think not insignificant, in the light of the fact that the great majority of them occur between the earlier and the later editions of the book rather than between the serial and the first edition. There are some twenty-five of these dialectic expressions, which, though they are identical in the serial, the first, and the fifth (English) editions, are modified and improved in the Osgood-M'Ilvaine Wessex edition of 1895. (This edition is, as I have said, presumably identical with the present Harper.)   Most obviously Hardy was again interested in making the dialect of his Wessex characters more distinctly their own, in preparation, I believe, for the Wessex edition.

As in *The Mayor* some of these changes are slight, the substitution of "en" or "'n" for "him," "ee" for "you," "be" for "are," but there are others more interesting.   I shall quote four of these, and hope that they will prove sufficient to convince the reader that Hardy made a conscious effort to strengthen and to improve the Wessex setting.   I place in brackets the words common to the serial and to the first and fifth editions.

From the confession of Tess to her mother:

"Why didn't you warn me?   Ladies know what to fend hands [guard] against, because they read novels that tell them of these tricks; but I never had the chance o' learning [of discovering] in that way, and you did not help me!"

Her mother was subdued.

"I thought if I spoke of his fond feelings and what they might lead to, you would *be hontish wi'* [dislike] him and lose your chance," she murmured, wiping her eyes with her apron. "Well, we must make the best of it, I suppose. 'Tis nater, after all, and what *do please* [pleases] God." [45]

From the conversation at the dairy over the slowness of the butter in coming:

" 'Tis years since I went to Conjuror Trendle's son in Egdon — years," said the dairyman, bitterly . . . "And I don't

believe in him. But I shall have to go to '*n* [him]. . . .
I shall have to go to '*n* [him] if this sort of thing continnys!"
. . . .

"Conjuror Fall, 'tother side of Casterbridge, . . . was
a very good man when I was a boy." said Jonathan Kail.
"But he's *rotten as touchwood by now* [dead and rotten]."

"My grandfather used to go to Conjuror Mynterne, . . .
and a clever man 'a were, so I've heard grandfer [grandfather]
say," continued Mr. Crick.[46]

From the meeting of Tess and Marian at Flintcomb-
Ash:

"Tess — Mrs. Clare — The dear wife of dear he! . . .
Why is you comely face tied up in such a way? Anybody been
beating 'ee?"

"No, no, no! I merely did it *to keep off clipsing and calling*
[not to be molested], Marian!"[47]

CERTAIN MINOR ADDITIONS AND ALTERATIONS

Under this general heading in the preceding chapter
I have presented certain passages which had been added
to the book version of *The Mayor of Casterbridge*,
obviously for the improvement of the literary atmosphere. There are more of these passages in *Tess* —
fourteen in all — which, absent in the serial, are with
one exception present in the earliest book edition and
in the ones succeeding. This fact helps to prove, I
think, my assumption in the introductory note to this
chapter, *i.e.* that, although the serial version may in
incident and plot represent a later modified form of
the story, the absence in it of passages which add dis-

tinct literary tone certainly bears witness that the original story (which Hardy claims was earlier than the
serial) was renovated before it was published in book
form in 1891.

I shall quote here four of these passages with the
necessary context, italicizing in each case the added
portions.[48]   The portions not italicized are common to
both serial and book versions:

(1) His host and his host's household, his men and his maids,
as they became intimately known to Clare, began to differenti-
ate themselves as in a chemical process. *The thought of Pas-
cal's was brought home to him. "A mesure qu'on a plus d'es-
prit, on trouve qu'il y a plus d'hommes originaux. Les gens du
commun ne trouvent pas de différence entre les hommes."* The
typical and unvarying Hodge ceased to exist. [49]

(2) Angel Clare had come as pupil to this dairy in the idea
that his temporary existence here was to be the merest episode
in his life, soon passed through and early forgotten; he had
come as to a place from which as from a screened alcove he
could calmly view the absorbing world surging without, and,
apostrophizing it with Walt Whitman —

> *Crowds of men and women attired in the usual costumes,
> How curious you are to me!* —

resolve upon a plan for plunging into that world anew.[50]

(3) Towards the second evening she reached the irregular
chalk table-land or plateau, bosomed [*pimpled* (in serial)] with
prehistoric semi-globular tumuli — *as if Cybele the Many-
breasted were supinely extended there* — which stretched between the valley of her birth and the valley of her love.[51]

(4) "He said at another time something like this"; and she
gave another, which might possibly have been paralleled in

many a work of the pedigree ranging from the Dictionnaire Philosophique to Huxley's Essays.[52]

In this presentation of minor additions and alterations, I must include also certain passages, present in the book but evidently to be numbered, in their absence from the serial, among those "slight modifications" made in the preparation of the magazine version. Among these passages are, first, those omitted from the serial in the desire not to offend the taste or jeopardize the morals of any reader; and second, those omitted because of their suggestion of skepticism or of lack of reverence toward existing forms of faith.

There are some dozen illustrations of the former, of which I shall quote three, using the same system of italicizing as in the quotation of the literary passages. The portions not italicized occur in both serial and book versions. Where it is necessary to show corresponding but differing passages in the serial, I have italicized those and placed them in brackets.

From the conversation between Joan and John Durbeyfield concerning the departure of Tess to work for Mrs. D'Urberville:

Joan Durbeyfield always managed to find consolation somewhere.

"Well, as one of the genuine stock, she ought to make her way with en, if she plays her trump card aright. *And if he don't marry her afore he will after. For that he's all afire wi'* love for her any eye can see." [53]

From Dairyman Crick's story of Jack Dollop:

"Well, how the woman should have had the wit to guess it I could never tell, but she found out that he was inside that there churn. Without saying a word she took hold of the winch (it was turned by hand-power then), and round she swung him, and Jack began to flop about inside. 'O Lord! stop the churn! let me out!' says he, popping out his head; 'I shall be churned into a pummy!' . . . 'Not till you make amend *for* [*trifling with her feelings!* (in serial)] *ravaging her trustful innocence!*' says the old woman. *'Stop the churn, you old witch!* screams he. '*You call me old witch, do ye, you deceiver,*' says she, *'when ye ought to ha' been calling me mother-in-law these last five months!*' *And on went the churn, and Jack's bones rattled round again.* Well, none of us ventured to interfere; and at last 'e promised to make it right *by marrying* [*wi'* (in serial)] her." [54]

From Tess's thoughts in regard to Clare's sense of responsibility toward the dairymaids:

Tess was woman enough to realize from their avowals to herself that Angel Clare had the honor of all the dairymaids in his keeping, and her perception of his care to avoid compromising the happiness of either in the least degree bred a tender respect in *Tess* [*her* (in serial)] for *what she deemed, rightly or wrongly, the self-controlling* [*the purity of mind and chivalrous* (in serial)] sense of duty shown by [*Angel Clare, qualities* (in serial)] *him, a quality* which she had never expected to find in one of the opposite sex, *and in the absence of which more than one of the simple hearts who were his housemates might have gone weeping on her pilgrimage.*[55]

There are fewer passages which suggest skepticism toward Church doctrine or existing forms of faith, but

those few are significant, in their omission from the
serial and their presence in the book versions. I quote
the most important, italicizing the portions absent from
the serial.

From the conversation between Angel and his father
as to the former's taking Orders in the Church:

"Since you have alluded to the matter, father," said the son,
with anxious thought upon his face, "I should like to say, once
for all, that I should prefer not to take Orders in the Church.
I fear I could not conscientiously do so. . . . There is no
institution for whose history I have a deeper admiration; but
I cannot honestly be ordained her minister, as my brothers are,
*while she refuses to liberate her mind from an untenable
redemptive theology.*

. . . .

*"My whole instinct in matters of religion is towards recon-
struction; to quote your favorite Epistle to the Hebrews, 'the
removing of those things that are shaken, as of things that are
made, that those things which cannot be shaken may remain.' "* [56]

From the conversation between Tess and Alec
D'Urberville, in regard to his newly-acquired religious
beliefs:

D'Urberville rose and came nearer, reclining sideways amid
the sheaves, and resting upon his elbow. "Since I last saw you,
I have been thinking of what you said HE said *about religion*.
I have come to the conclusion that there does seem rather a
want of common sense in *the propitiatory scheme* [*my proposi-
tions* (in serial)]."

. . . .

"Hang it, I am not going to feel responsible for my deeds and passions any more, *if there's nobody to be responsible to."*   . . .

She tried to argue and tell him that he had mixed in his dull brain two distinct matters, *theology and morals,* which *in the primitive days of mankind had been quite distinct* and had nothing in common but long association.[57]

In addition to these alterations there are others which deserve at least a comment. There is evident on the part of the serial author an aversion to profanity. In several instances the profanity, which stands quite unglossed in the book, is omitted from the serial entirely or much softened. For instance, Angel in the serial refrains from uttering the name of "God" in an ejaculation, and Alec D'Urberville, though he swears by "God" in the book, uses "Heaven" for that purpose in the serial. Moreover, when Tess catches his arm in the window hinge, he merely cries, "Confound it!" in the serial, whereas "Damnation!" is his exclamation in the book. Even in the first edition, as well as in the serial, Angel Clare refrains from telling Tess that "a certain place is paved with good intentions." Twice in the serial is "Providence" substituted for "God."

Slight as these changes are, they most certainly reveal the attitude of many readers of the late Victorian era. Doubtless the pendulum today has swung too far in the other direction, since neither author nor editor must guard the morals and religious beliefs of a public which scorns the didactic and demands the risqué. And yet it is not difficult to imagine the amused leniency with which Hardy consented to make such alterations.

CHANGES IN DICTION, GRAMMAR, AND SENTENCE STRUCTURE

It is often alleged by Hardy readers that *Tess of the D'Urbervilles*, more than any other of his novels, claimed Hardy's interest and sympathy. Whether this contention be true or not, it can at least be truly said that Hardy expended more care upon the details of *Tess* than upon any other of the four novels which show distinct alterations from one version to another. This care is shown especially in the changes in diction, particularly in word substitutions, of which there are nearly three hundred. The majority of these occur in the changes from the serial to the first edition, for I am assuming, as I announced in the introductory note, that these obvious improvements in diction and sentence structure bear witness to the fact that the first form of the story, not improved in these details for serial publication, was altered before the publication of the first edition. There are several of these substitutions, however, which in a given instance occur in the revision of the serial for the first edition, and again in the revision of the first for the later editions. For example, the word "crime" in the serial becomes "dislike" in the first, and "aversion" in the Harper edition.[58] Again there are many instances of the substitution of one word for another between the first edition and the Harper,[59] when no change occurs between the serial and the first.[60] Finally there are several instances of a word changed from serial to book, and then back

again to the serial form in the Harper edition.[61]   All
these alterations, I think, go to prove that Hardy ex-
perimented more carefully with his diction in *Tess* than
in the other novels under discussion, in his search for
the most forceful, specific, and suggestive words.

It is quite impossible to give many examples of these
various substitutions.   The few I am quoting are char-
acteristic of all — that is, they give evidence of a care-
fulness of detail on the part of Hardy, and do, in almost every case, prove themselves better words than
those whose position they have taken.

First, in the serial the pleasure which Angel Clare
takes in the life at Talbothays Dairy is described as
"æsthetic, *idealistic*, pagan"; in the book, as "æsthetic,
sensuous, pagan." [62]

Second, in the serial Tess, dressing for her wedding,
"moved about in a mental cloud of many-colored *ideal-
isms*, which eclipsed all *commonplaces* by its own iri-
descence"; in the book, she "moved about in a mental
cloud of many-colored *idealities*, which eclipsed all
sinister contingencies by its *brightness*." [63]

Third, the turnip-slicing machine at Flintcomb-Ash
"in its bright blue hue of new paint" seemed, in the
serial, "*strange* in the otherwise colorless scene"; in the
book it seemed "*almost vocal.*" [64]

Conscious care is also evidenced in the correction of
grammar and in the improvement of several sentences
in the revision of the serial version, or of the first form
of the story, for the first edition.   One is tempted to
ask, it is true, why Hardy should ever have been care-

less enough to allow such lapses. The answer to such a question may presumably be that his birth and education did not afford him constant security against such mistakes.

Two mistakes in grammar occur in the serial version but are corrected in the first edition:

The single ale-house at this end of . . . the village *could only boast* of an off-license [(*could boast of only*) in the book].[65]

In addition to Tess, Marian, and Izz, there were two women from a neighboring village . . . *who* [*whom,* in the book] Tess with a start remembered as Dark Car, the Queen of Spades, and her junior, the Queen of Diamonds.[66]

There are ten instances of sentences rewritten in the revision for the first edition. These include sentences weak in reference, in unity, and coherence. I am quoting two of them in their original and in their revised form.

(1) From the serial: "In these early days of her residence here Tess did not skim, *going out of doors* at once after rising, where he was generally awaiting her."

From the book: "In these early days of her residence here Tess did not skim, *but went out of doors* at once after rising, where he was generally awaiting her." [67]

(2) From the serial: "He . . . hated Saint James as much as he dared, and regarded Timothy and Titus *with mixed feelings.*"

From the book: "He . . . hated Saint James as much as he dared, and regarded *with mixed feelings* Timothy, Titus, and Philemon." [68]

NOTES

[1] See chapters x and xi in Harper edition.

[2] Chapter ix in the book but x in the serial, in which the chapters are arranged somewhat differently, especially in the case of chapter iv, which in the serial becomes chapters iv and v.

[3] For change in position of this material and for alterations in it, see pages 66 and 80 of the annotated book.

[4] A. P. Webb, *A Bibliography of the Works of Thomas Hardy*, p. 62.

[5] It has been impossible to secure the *National Observer* for Nov. 14, 1891, and I cannot, therefore, be sure that the story is identical with chapters x and xi of the book. But since "The Midnight Baptism," which appeared in the *Fortnightly Review* for May, 1891, and which, except for obviously necessary omissions, is practically identical with chapter xiv of the book (omitted from the serial) I think I am safe in assuming that the story in the *National Observer* is, in its main outlines at least, identical with chapters x and xi. "The Midnight Baptism" exists quite by itself and does not use the names of the novel characters. This is, I think, without doubt true of "Saturday Night in Arcady."

[6] See p. 87 in Harper edition.

[7] For this incident, the departure of Tess and the meeting with the painter, see Harper edition, chapter xii, pp. 81-88.

[8] See page 76.

[9] It is interesting to note here that the italicized material does not occur in the first edition, though otherwise the passage in that edition is practically identical with that in the Harper.

[10] See pp. 89-90 in Harper edition.

[11] For this material see the *Graphic*, vol. 44, p. 136, or p. 89 of the annotated book in the University of Minnesota library.

[12] See note 9 above. This material is not in the first edition, and I am unable to say in what edition it first appeared. It is in the fifth English edition and in the standard Harper.

[13] See chapter xiv in Harper edition, pp. 94-108.

[14] See chapter lii in Harper edition, pp. 414-418.

[15] *Graphic*, vol. 44, p. 162, or p. 113 of the annotated book.

[16] See pp. 159-164 in Harper edition.

[17] See pp. 161-162 of the annotated book.

18 It is interesting to note that this italicized passage is absent from the first edition.

19 Again it is interesting to note that in the first edition "be" is substituted for "live." Apparently Hardy retained something of the caution evidenced in the serial.

20 See pp. 307-309 in Harper edition.

21 See pp. 307-308 of the annotated book.

22 See pp. 384-386 in Harper edition.

23 *Ibid.*, pp. 387 ff.

24 See p. 387 of the annotated book.

25 See p. 389 in Harper edition.

26 *Ibid.*, p. 390.

27 *Graphic*, vol. 44, p. 665, or the annotated book p. 392.

28 See p. 409 in the Harper edition.

29 *Ibid.*, p. 425.

30 See p. 425 of annotated book.

31 *Ibid.*, p 416.

32 *Ibid.*, p. 432.

33 The italicized sentences are absent from the first edition, though they are in the fifth English edition as they are in the Harper.

34 See p. 434 in Harper edition.

35 See p. 434 of the annotated book.

36 *Ibid.*, p. 436.

37 *Ibid.*, p. 437.

38 *Ibid.*, p. 10,

39 *Ibid.*, p. 84.

40 *Ibid.*, p. 271. It is interesting to note that this word appears also in the same place in the first edition.

41 *Ibid.*, p. 272.

42 *Ibid.*, p. 272. This also appears in the first edition. It is impossible to say just when it gave place to the following substitution.

43 *Ibid.*

44 It is to be noted here, I think, that *Tess* is far more rich in geography than is *The Mayor*, even in parts of the story which do not demand it. Might it not well be that by 1891, the year of the publication of *Tess* both in serial and book, Hardy had already begun to strengthen his Wessex atmosphere, and had decided upon his principal localities? As I pointed out in the discussion on setting in *The*

Mayor, the towns named in *Tess* are also suggestive of other Hardy stories.

[45] See p. 90 of the annotated book. This is, of course, not in the serial, as most of the incident is omitted. (See discussion of incident seven, page 78), but it does occur in the first and fifth editions.

[46] See p. 149 of the annotated book.

[47] *Ibid.*, p. 322.

[48] The other passages may be found on the following pages of the Harper edition: 9, 37, 92, 109, 263, 265, 299, 372, 392, and 451.

[49] See p. 132 of Harper edition.

[50] *Ibid.*, p. 173.

[51] See p. 321 in Harper edition. The reference to "Cybele, the Many-breasted" is absent not only from the serial but also from the first edition. Hardy continued to add literary tone!

[52] *Ibid.*, p. 368.

[53] *Ibid.*, p. 55.

[54] *Ibid.*, p. 150.

[55] *Ibid.*, p. 158.

[56] *Ibid.*, pp. 128-129.

[57] *Ibid.*, pp. 377-378.

[58] See p. 388 of the annotated book.

[59] It is obviously impossible to tell just when this later substitution occurs, since the editions (except the fifth) between the first and the Harper are not procurable. The fifth is identical in this instance with the Harper.

[60] An example of this occurs on p. 42 of the annotated book. In both serial and first edition Tess eats "in an abstracted, half-hypnotised state"; in the Harper edition, "in a half-pleased, half-reluctant state."

[61] This is shown on p. 402 of the annotated book. In the serial, "D'Urberville went away from her"; in the first, he "retreated"; in the Harper again he "went away from her."

[62] See p. 178 of the annotated book.

[63] *Ibid.*, p. 241.

[64] *Ibid.*, p. 358.

[65] *Ibid.*, p. 22.

[66] *Ibid.*, p. 331.

[67] *Ibid.*, p. 146.

[68] *Ibid.*, p. 178.

JUDE THE OBSCURE

JUDE THE OBSCURE

J UDE the Obscure is one of the five first editions of
Thomas Hardy's works published in the Wessex
Novels edition by Osgood, M'ILvaine and Company in
1895, and taken over two years later by Harper and
Brothers.[1] As I have stated in the introduction to this
study, this first edition of *Jude* is, with the exception of
changes from English to American spelling, identical
with the present standard Harper version. There is,
therefore, in the discussion of this one novel no question of alterations made from edition to edition. We
have to consider, then, simply the changes made from
serial to book, or, as the case may be, from book to
serial.

In his preface to the first edition, the preface quoted
in the present standard version of the story, Hardy
gives us the history of the novel:

"The history of this novel (whose birth in its present
shape has been much retarded by the necessities of periodical publication) is briefly as follows. The scheme
was jotted down in 1890, from notes made in 1887 and
onward, some of the circumstances being suggested by
the death of a woman in the former year. The scenes
were revisited in October, 1892; the narrative was
written in outline in 1892 and the spring of 1893, and
at full length, as it now appears, from August, 1893,

onward into the next year; the whole, with the exception of a few changes, being in the hands of the publisher by the end of 1894.   It was begun as a serial
story in *Harper's Magazine* at the end of November,
1894, and was continued in monthly parts.

"But, as in the case of *Tess of the D'Urbervilles*,
the magazine version was, for various reasons, abridged
and modified in some degree, the present edition being
the first in which the whole appears as originally written.   And in the difficulty of coming to an early decision
in the matter of title, the tale was issued under a pro-
visional name — two such titles having, in fact, been
successively adopted.[2]   The present and final title,
deemed on the whole the best, was one of the earliest
thought of."

From Hardy's own statement, then, we are to infer,
as in the case of *Tess*, first, that the book form of the
story is older than the serial; and second, that that
form was "abridged and modified in some degree" for
serial publication.   The statement is easy to accept, so
far as the incidents of the novel are concerned.   The
plot of the story, as we know it today, is without doubt
identical with that of the original form, and the alterations apparent in the serial version were obviously
made at the request of the editor of *Harper's*, who
feared lest he shock the sensibilities of his readers.
But, also as in the case of *Tess*, there are evidences of
improvements made in the diction and in the sentence
structure of the book over those of the serial, improvements which show, I think, that the original form of

the story was revised in these particulars before its publication in book form.

I make, therefore, the same assumption which I made in the case of *Tess of the D'Urbervilles*: that the original version of *Jude the Obscure* was, in incident and plot, the story as we know it today; that that version was modified in incident and plot to suit the editor of *Harper's Magazine*; and finally, that, to make it ready for book publication, it was improved in diction, in sentence structure, and, to a slight degree, by the addition of references contributing a literary tone and atmosphere.

CHANGES IN INCIDENT AND PLOT

I shall proceed in this chapter of my study exactly as I have done in the two preceding: I shall summarize the story of *Jude the Obscure*, as it is known to all Hardy readers from the present standard Harper version, by giving as briefly as possible the main incidents of that story. Again I shall star those incidents most significant to this study because of the different treatment accorded them in the serial version.

The summary of the story, then, is as follows:

1. Richard Phillotson, the schoolmaster of Marygreen, leaves the village for Christminster, the University town, warning Jude Fawley, a boy of ten, to be kind to animals, to read, and not to forget him.

2. Jude, the grandnephew of Drusilla Fawley, baker, follows the schoolmaster's instructions, and, as

he grows older, conceives a great passion for learning and for Christminster.

3. As he drives the baker's wagon and delivers bread for his aunt, he studies the classics and continues to dream of Christminster.

4. At the age of nineteen, when returning home one Saturday from Alfredston, in which place he has apprenticed himself to a stonecutter, he meets Arabella Donn, the daughter of a pig-breeder.

*5. Arabella entices him to leave his studies for her society, and finally, upon the advice of some friends of hers and of the quack physician Vilbert, succeeds two months later in drawing him into marriage with her on the plea that a child is coming.

*6. After a few months of discordant married life, during which Jude discovers not only that no child is coming, but that his Christminster dreams have been shattered by his marriage, they separate, Arabella going to Australia with her parents.

7. Jude goes to Christminster, obtains work as a stonemason, dreams again of entering one of the colleges in the future, and meets his cousin Sue Bridehead, a clever, unorthodox young woman, to whom he is instantly attracted.

8. Through Jude's renewed friendship with Richard Phillotson, whom he discovers through Sue in a nearby village and still a schoolmaster, Sue Bridehead becomes Phillotson's assistant.

*9. Jude writes to five learned doctors to ask their opinion of his chances at entering one of the colleges, and receives a reply from only one, and that reply discouraging.

10. Disheartened at the letter and at his own realization of the futility of his plans, Jude drinks heavily, loses his position, goes back to Marygreen, and finally, giving up his Christminster dreams, decides to train at Melchester, a cathedral town, to enter the Church as a licentiate.

11. Sue, who is attending a teachers' training school at Melchester, tells Jude of her engagement to Phillotson, and of their plans for marriage after two years.

12. Sue and Jude go for a walk, unfortunately miss the last train home, and are obliged to stay for the night with an old shepherd and his wife.

13. For this offence Sue is placed in solitary confinement, from which she escapes one evening and goes to Jude, who cares for her until morning when she goes to the house of a friend.

14. Jude finds himself completely in love with Sue, realizes the hopelessness of his situation, and tells her of his early marriage with Arabella.

15. Apparently piqued by Jude's story, Sue informs him a few days later that she and Phillotson are to be married in a few weeks, and asks Jude to give her away.

*16. A few weeks after the wedding Jude meets Arabella in a Christminster inn, is easily induced by her to spend the night with her at Aldbrickham, a nearby town, and finds out the morning after that she has married a man in Australia.

17. Sue and Jude go to Marygreen upon the death of their great-aunt Drusilla, and there Sue confesses to Jude that she cannot endure to live with Phillotson as his wife.

18. Jude, recognizing his love for Sue and its inconsistency with his plans to enter the Church, decides that, in order to be honest, he must give up those plans, and accordingly burns his religious books in his Aunt Drusilla's garden.

*19. Sue, having left Phillotson's bed for the clothes-closet, confesses her aversion to him, and asks him to release her in order that she may go to Jude.

20. Phillotson, who honestly believes that it is wrong to torture his wife and that the mere ceremony of marriage does not constitute a union, consents to Sue's request, in spite of contrary advice from his friend Gillingham, a fellow schoolmaster.

*21. Sue leaves Phillotson and goes to Jude, who takes her to Aldbrickham, where they will be unknown, and who learns to his surprise that she does not, for the present at least, intend to live with him as his wife.

*22. Sue and Jude get lodgings in Aldbrickham, but they do not live together as man and wife, even though Jude's divorce of Arabella and Phillotson's of Sue are granted.

*23. Arabella comes to Aldbrickham in distress and finds Jude, who in spite of Sue's objections wishes to help her, and who desists only when Sue consents to give herself entirely to him.

24. Sue and Jude now plan to marry, but are de-

terred by the fear that marriage will destroy their love. This fear has been engendered by their great-aunt Drusilla's tales of the unfortunate marriages in their family.

25. Arabella writes Jude of their son born in Australia eight months after their separation, and Jude and Sue decide to take the boy, who proves to be a strange child, old beyond his years.

*26. Jude and Sue again attempt marriage, but cannot carry it out. Their neighbors begin to speculate as to their relations and as to the identity of the child, and finally, when Sue's first child is about to come, they (Sue and Jude) decide they must move elsewhere.

27. After nearly three years of moving from place to place, Jude falls ill, and is cared for by Sue and an old Marygreen friend, the Widow Edlin.

*28. Sue is discovered selling Christminster cakes at Kennetbridge fair by Arabella, whose husband has died and who has become, through sudden conversion, a chapel-goer.

29. After her conversation with Sue concerning Jude, Arabella forgets her conversion, and allows her old passion for Jude to reassert itself.

30. Upon Jude's partial recovery, he and Sue return to Christminster with Jude's boy and their own two children.

*31. They find difficulty in getting lodgings, and their discouragement affects the boy, who talks with Sue and to whom she confides the news that there is soon to be another child.

*32. The boy, left alone for a time, hangs the two younger children to a nail on the door, and then hangs himself.

*33. Sue, almost deranged, goes to the cemetery alone after the burial, tries to induce the man filling in the grave to allow her to see the children once more, is coaxed home by Jude, and shortly afterward gives birth to a still-born child.

34. Sue, convalescent, begins to go to church again, and finally conceives the idea that she is married to Phillotson and to him alone.

*35. She sends Jude away from her, refusing to live again with him as his wife.

*36. Phillotson, hearing from Arabella that Sue and Jude are no longer living together, writes to Sue and asks her to come back to him.

*37. Sue returns to Phillotson, and is remarried to him in the church at Marygreen.

*38. Arabella searches for Jude, forces herself upon him by representing herself as penniless, induces him to drink, and finally takes him home with her, with the result that a few days later he marries her.

*39. Jude, now ill, goes one afternoon to Marygreen and sends for Sue, who meets him in the church, where they again confess their love for each other.

*40. Although advised to the contrary by the Widow Edlin, Sue, to do penance for her sin of confessing her love for Jude, goes that night to her husband's room, tells him of her meeting with Jude, swears on the New

Testament that she will never see him again, and asks Phillotson to take her as his wife.

*41. Jude, dying at Christminster, is visited by Mrs. Edlin with news of Sue.

*42. Arabella prepares for her future by inveigling the physician Vilbert.

*43. Jude dies alone while Arabella goes to the boat-races, and two days later lies in his coffin, Arabella and Mrs. Edlin beside him, and the voices of the Doctors conferring degrees coming through the open window.

Now to the discussion of the starred incidents. How were they "abridged and modified" for serial publication? For "abridged and modified" they surely were, and more than "in some degree."

The first important difference in treatment is seen in the handling of incident five — in which Arabella Donn, acting upon the advice of some wise friends of hers, successfully brings about her marriage with Jude. It is unnecessary to comment upon the importance of these events to the story as a whole. They obviously form the motivating incident upon which the novel is based. A brief summary will be sufficient for the recalling of the details of the incident as they are given in the book:

Arabella, determined to win Jude at any cost, accepts the advice of her friends Sarah and Anny, who tell her to entice Jude into intimacy with her until she discovers herself pregnant, whereupon she can insist upon marriage. Her first attempt is unsuccessful; her second, however, successfully begins their intimacy. Two months later, after repeated meetings with her lover, and after some necessary assurance from an itinerant quack named Vilbert, Arabella informs Jude, who has just announced his intention of going away from her, that a child is coming. He thereupon agrees with her that they must marry at once.

In order to see clearly the changes made in the serial version it is necessary to present separately each step of the incident. In the first place, the advice of Arabella's friends is very different in the serial from what it is in the book. The changes made in the serial are most easily seen by a comparison of the two passages dealing with the advice.

From the book:

In a few moments Arabella replied in a curiously low, fierce tone of latent sensuousness: "I've got him to care for me — yes! But I want him to more than care for me; I want him to have me — to marry me! I must have him. I can't do without him. He's the sort of man I long for. I shall go mad if I can't give myself to him altogether! I felt I should when I first saw him!"

"As he is a romancing, straightfor'ard, honest chap, he's to be had, and as a husband, if you set about catching him in the right away."

Arabella remained thinking a while. "What med be the right way?" she asked.

"Oh, you don't know — you don't!" said Sarah, the third girl.

"On my word, I don't!—No further, that is, than by plain courting, and taking care he don't go too far!"

The third girl looked at the second. "She don't know!"

" 'Tis clear she don't!" said Anny.

"And having lived in a town, too, as one may say! Well, we can teach 'ee som'at, then, as well as you us."

"Yes. And how do you mean — a sure way to gain a man? Take me for a innocent, and have done wi' it!"

"As a husband?"

"As a husband."

"A countryman that's honorable and serious-minded such as he. God forbid that I should say a sojer or sailor, or commercial gent from the towns, or any of them that be slippery with poor women! I'd do no friend that harm!"

"Well, such as he, of course!"

* Arabella's companions looked at each other, and, turning up their eyes in drollery, began smirking. Then one went up close to Arabella, and, although nobody was near, imparted some information in a low tone, the other observing curiously the effect upon Arabella.

"Ah!" said the last-named slowly. "I own I didn't think of that way! . . . But suppose he isn't honorable? A woman had better not have tried it!"

"Nothing venture, nothing have! Besides, you make sure he's honorable before you begin. You'd be safe enough with yours. I wish I had the chance! Lots of girls do it, or do you think they'd get married at all?"

Arabella pursued her way in silent thought. "I'll try it!" she whispered, but not to them.[3]

The accounts in book and serial are practically identical from the beginning to the place marked (*)

"Arabella's companions." From there the serial account runs as follows:

Arabella's companions nodded.

"The plan is," said the one who had spoken last, "to invent another young man that you've thrown over for him, though he's willing to have you back again. And you show the letter."

"Show the letter?"

"Yes, the letter from him offering to marry you right off. I'll write it for 'ee. You could do it easily as you have been away to Aldbrickham. You could say he lives there and courted you there. You must tell it trembling, and have a good watery cry."

"Ah!" said Arabella, smiling. "I own I didn't think of it! . . . But suppose he finds out 'tisn't true? A woman had better not have tried it then."

"Nothing venture, nothing have! You'd be safe enough in your case. I wish I had the chance! Lots of girls have to play such tricks, or do you think they'd get married at all?"

Arabella pursued her way in silent thought. "I'll try it!" she whispered, but not to them.[4]

Even a hasty comparison will serve, I think, to convince the reader that the serial account is a makeshift and a poor one at that. The advice here given by Arabella's friends is certainly not the kind that would demand such a mysterious introduction, with its references to "them that be slippery with poor women," following which introduction the advice itself is a decided anti-climax. It is, indeed, the first of many makeshifts which the editor of *Harper's* apparently thought must be made, even at a tremendous sacrifice of plausibility and of art, in order that the taste and the sense of propriety of his readers might not be offended.

The same care is shown in the serial treatment of Arabella's first attempt to induce Jude to marry her. (Surely her behavior in the serial is too decorous to be termed "enticing"!) Again I think it is best to quote both episodes (*i.e.* from the book and then from the serial), so that the contrast between them may be clearly seen.

The preliminary material is the same in both accounts. Jude, coming home on Saturday evening from Alfredston, finds upon his arrival at Arabella's that three pigs have escaped from their sty. He assists Arabella in attempting to catch them, and in a futile chase they run at some distance across the downs. Finally they find themselves alone on the summit of a hill — "in absolute solitude." The account in the book continues:

Without relinquishing her hold of Jude's hand she swerved aside and flung herself down on the sod under a stunted thorn, precipitately pulling Jude on to his knees at the same time.

"Oh, I ask pardon — I nearly threw you down, didn't I? But I am so tired!"

She lay supine, and straight as an arrow, on the sloping sod of this hill-top, gazing up into the blue miles of sky, and still retaining her warm hold of Jude's hand. He reclined on his elbow near her.

"We've run all this way for nothing," she went on, her form heaving and falling in quick pants, her face flushed, her full

red lips parted, and a fine dew of perspiration on her skin.
"Well — why don't you speak, deary?"

"I'm blown too. It was all up hill."

They were in absolute solitude — the most apparent of all
solitudes, that of empty surrounding space. Nobody could be
nearer than a mile to them without their seeing him. They
were, in fact, on one of the summits of the county, and the
distant landscape around Christminster could be discerned from
where they lay. But Jude did not think of that then.

"Oh, I can see such a pretty thing up this tree," said Arabella.
"A sort of a — caterpillar, of the most loveliest green and
yellow you ever came across!"

"Where?" said Jude, sitting up.

"You can't see him there — you must come here," said she.

He bent nearer and put his head by hers. "No — I can't
see it," he said.

"Why, on the limb there where it branches off — close to the
moving leaf — there!" She gently pressed his face towards
the position.

"I don't see it," he repeated, the back of his head against her
cheek. "But I can, perhaps, standing up." He stood accordingly, placing himself in the direct line of her gaze.

"How stupid you are!" she said crossly, turning away her
face.

"I don't care to see it, dear; why should I?" he replied, looking down upon her. "Get up, Abby."

"Why?"

"I want you to let me kiss you. I've been waiting to ever so
long!"

She rolled round her face, remained a moment looking deed-
ily aslant at him; then, with a slight curl to the lip, sprang to

her feet, and exclaiming abruptly, "I must mizzle!" walked off quickly homeward. Jude followed and rejoined her.

"Just one!" he coaxed.

"Shan't!" she said.

He, surprised: "What's the matter?"

She kept her two lips resentfully together, and Jude followed her like a pet lamb till she slackened her pace and walked beside him, talking calmly on indifferent subjects, and always checking him if he tried to take her hand or clasp her waist. Thus they descended to the precincts of her father's homestead, and Arabella went in, nodding good-bye to him with a supercilious, affronted air.

"I expect I took too much liberty with her somehow," Jude said to himself, as he withdrew with a sigh and went on to Marygreen.⁵

Now in the serial account Arabella's behavior is far more decorous. She does not lie down; accordingly, she does not attempt to bring Jude beside her by the feint of throwing him down. Nor does she attempt to bring him nearer her by trying to make him see the caterpillar. All of these details, which in the book give such consistency to the character of Arabella as we already know it, are omitted from the magazine version. Instead, following the advice of her friends as given in the serial, she tells him of the Aldbrickham young man:

Relinquishing her hold of Jude's hands as if with relief, she sat down on the sod under a stunted thorn, and remained some time in reverie, her form heaving and falling in quick pants, her face flushed, her full red lips parted, and a fine dew of perspiration upon her skin. Jude stood before her, looking sometimes into the distance, sometimes back into her face.

"You look tired, dear," he said.

"I am not so very tired; only out o' breath," she murmured.

"You seem out of spirits, or something, then. What is it?" He bent down to kiss her.

"No, Jude; you mustn't. It has to do with that. I mean what makes me seem down and melancholy. I've got to tell 'ee; and I don't like to."

"But do, Arabella," he urged anxiously.

She looked far away at the solitude which was absolute. They were, in fact, on one of the summits of the country, and could discern the remote landscape around Christminster (which Jude did not think of as being attractive then), till she glanced gloomily at her pocket, and other hand that held something white partially withdrawn from it.

"What have you there?" said he.

"A letter. Oh, never mind." She thrust the letter back into her pocket again.

"Is it that which troubles you?"

"Yes, partly. I don't know how to answer it."

"I cannot advise you unless I know what it is about."

"And if I tell you, you'll be angry with me."

"I promise not to be."

"Very well, then. It is about another young man."

"Another?" Jude felt the beginning of a cold sweat supervening on his hot one. Till this moment Arabella had never hinted a word of another lover, or done anything to cause him the least jealousy.

"When I was at Aldbrickham," she went on, "I was followed up by two or three; and one in particular I rather liked.

He was a rather nice young gentleman, and is still. Oh, I did serve him bad, poor chap!"

"Why was that?"

"How stupid you be!" she said crossly. "I came home, and then I saw you, and — gave him the cold shoulder —"

"You were a dear."

"But that isn't all. He forgives everything; offers to marry me off-hand, even now, if I'll say yes. To think that he is so constant, after all! I don't deserve it. I am unworthy of such."

She drew out the letter and unfolded it, expecting Jude to ask to see it. He merely said, "Is that the offer of marriage?"

"Yes," said she.

Jude sighed. "Of course," he said mournfully, "if you think so much about him, and think you ought to have him, I must bear the loss of you. But I didn't expect such a blow as this. However, I won't reproach you. But as long as I live I shall never forget you. I was going to ask for one last kiss. Perhaps I have no right to. You ought to have told me of this before . . . so I am to take it as being all over between us?"

Arabella remained a moment longer, looking nettled, then, with a slight curl of her lip, she sprang to her feet, and exclaiming abruptly, "I must mizzle!" walked off quickly homeward. Jude followed heavily and rejoined her.

"Just one!" he coaxed, "though I ought not, I suppose, now?"

"Shan't!" she said.

He, surprised and hurt: "You needn't answer like that, dear, even if I did ask for what I have no longer a right to expect. I didn't know till now —"

She kept her two lips resentfully together, and Jude followed her like a pet lamb till she slackened her pace and walked beside him, talking calmly on indifferent subjects. Then they descended to the precincts of her father's homestead, and Arabella went in, merely nodding good-bye to him with a supercilious, affronted air.

"Shall I see you once more?" he faltered.

"Yes, once, if you like. Sunday evening," said she, with suppressed ire.

"I ought not to have tried to kiss her after what she had told me," Jude murmured sadly as he went on to Marygreen.[6]

Arabella's second, and this time successful, attempt to capture Jude as given in the book, consistent as it is with her nature and necessary as the motivating incident of the tragedy that follows — the tragedy of Jude's weakness, which *is* the story — apparently proved too bald and too bold for the editor of *Harper's* to give to his readers with impunity. Accordingly, since he would have none of it, the author rearranged his story so that the incident of the bantam's egg, with its culminating episode in a chamber of the Donn house, might be entirely omitted from the serial. In its place he substituted Arabella's announcement to Jude of the letter of acceptance, which she has written to her Aldbrickham lover, and Jude's passionate declaration of his own readiness to marry her, following which declaration he tears up the letter.

The following excerpts show clearly the contrasting incidents in their relation to each other. In both book and serial the narrative leading up to the incidents is in all important respects the same. Jude and Arabella go for a walk, and come back home in the early evening.

From the book:

In-doors they went. Did he want any tea? No, it was too late; he would rather sit and talk to her. She took off her jacket and hat, and they sat down — naturally enough close together.

"Don't touch me, please," she said softly. "I am part eggshell; or perhaps I had better put it in a safe place." She began unfastening the collar of her gown.

"What is it?" said her lover.

"An egg — a bantam's egg. I am hatching a very rare sort. I carry it about everywhere with me, and it will get hatched in less than three weeks."

"Where do you carry it?"

"Just here." She put her hand into her bosom and drew out the egg, which was wrapped in wool, outside it being a piece of pig's bladder, in case of accidents. Having exhibited it to him, she put it back. "Now, mind, you don't come near me. I don't want to get it broke, and have to begin another."

"Why do you do such a strange thing?"

"Just for a fancy. I suppose it is natural for a woman to want to bring live things into the world."

"It is very awkward for me just now," he said laughing.

"It serves you right. There — that's all you can have of me." She had turned round her chair, and reaching over the back of it presented her cheek to him gingerly.

"That's very shabby of you!"

"You should have catched me a minute ago when I had put the egg down! There!" she said, defiantly, "I am without it now!" She had quickly withdrawn the egg a second time; but before he could quite reach her she had put it back as quickly, laughing with the excitement of her strategy. Then there was a little struggle, Jude making a plunge for it and capturing it triumphantly. Her face flushed; and becoming suddenly conscious, he flushed also.

They looked at each other, panting; till he rose and said: "One kiss; now I can do it without damage to property, and I'll go!"

But she had jumped up too. "You must find me first!" she cried.

Her lover followed her as she withdrew. It was now dark inside the room, and the window being small, he could not discover for a long time what had become of her, till a laugh revealed her to have rushed up the stair, whither Jude rushed at her heels.[7]

From the serial:

Indoors they went. She asked, listlessly, if he wanted tea? No, he did not care about it; he would rather sit and talk to her.

She sank down in a chair, remained silent for a minute or so, and then burst into tears.

"What is it?" said Jude, much distressed.

"He's coming!" she said. "Look on the chimley-piece!"

He looked, and saw a letter, directed to a man at Aldbrickham whose name was strange to him, in Arabella's handwriting.

"What is it — acceptance of him?" said Jude, pale as death.

"I've been drove to it!" she sobbed. "He says he shall come for me willy-nilly and father and mother say I must have him! But I don't want to — because — I love you best! But I must give you up, because you be not ready, and he is!"

"I am ready!" said Jude, passionately. "I can't let you go! Tell your father and mother that I am as ready as he! When is he coming?"

"He tells father he's coming in three weeks."

"We'll be married by that time! Will you tear up that letter?"

"Will you? It will mean to father and mother that you take his place if I tell them you tore it up."

Jude rushed and tore up the letter, and kissed her more than once; and she said, with real gladness, "And you won't desert me?" [8]

The last step in this long but very important incident — Arabella's conference with Vilbert and her announcement to Jude that a child is coming — is entirely omitted from the serial, necessarily of course, since according to that story Jude and Arabella have not indulged themselves in intimacy and since Jude is marrying her because he cannot bear to give her up to the Aldbrickham lover. The following quotation from the book gives this last step in Arabella's successful capture:

It was some two months later in the year, and the pair had met constantly during the interval. Arabella seemed dissatisfied; she was always imagining and waiting and wondering.

One day she met the itinerant Vilbert. She, like all the cottagers thereabout, knew the quack well, and they began talking about her experiences. Arabella had been gloomy, but before he left her she had grown brighter. That evening she kept an appointment with Jude, who seemed sad.

"I am going away," he said to her. "I think I ought to go. I think it will be better both for you and for me. I wish some things had never begun! I was much to blame, I know. But it is never too late to mend."

Arabella began to cry. "How do you know it is not too late?" she said. "That's all very well to say! I haven't told you yet!" and she looked into his face with streaming eyes.

"What?" he asked, turning pale. "Not —?"

"Yes! And what shall I do if you desert me?"

"Oh, Arabella — how can you say that, my dear! You know I wouldn't desert you!" [9]

I have felt it necessary to treat thus exhaustively this initial incident of the novel for the simple fact that it is the motivating force of the story. Upon Jude's passion for Arabella and his unfortunate marriage with her hang most of the disaster of his career: the shattering of his dreams of Christminster; the tragedy of his love for Sue, who, upon hearing of Jude's disastrous marriage, hastens her own disastrous union with Phillotson; the awful catastrophe of the murder of the children of Sue and Jude by the son of Jude and Arabella, who follows murder by suicide — all these and more hark directly back to this first great mishap. How necessary, then, that this all-important incident should be consistently treated, as it is in the book! Arabella is assuredly a "low-passioned woman," [10] from the hour when she throws the piece of the pig at Jude to attract his attention to the hour when she, knowing that Jude is dying, casts dangerous eyes upon Vilbert. She is not a woman who will play the silly trick of a ficticious letter in order to capture a lover when another and far more satisfactory means is at hand. Nor is

the Jude of the serial any more consistent. We are
told in the serial, as in the book, that Jude "knew well
. . . that Arabella was not worth a great deal as
a specimen of womankind." [11] Why then does he marry
her? There is only *one* adequate reason — the one
given in the book: he has "drifted so far into intimacy
with her that he must take the consequences." [12] Surely,
feeling as he does about her, he will not marry her
merely to keep her from another lover, as he is made
to do in the serial version.

The disastrous marriage of Jude with Arabella is
the starting-point and keynote of his tragic career. It
is motivated by his weakness and by her passion. What
a frightful sacrifice of consistency in characterization
and of plausibility in plot are entailed by the alterations
in the serial version!

Other necessary alterations are made in the serial in
the treatment of incident six — Jude's discovery that
no child is coming and their separation after a few
months of discordant married life — since in the magazine version the motivation for their marriage is different.

In the book we are first told that no child is coming
by a conversation between Arabella and her advisor
Anny. The conversation runs in this wise:

As usual, they laughed before talking; the world seemed
funny to them without saying it.

"So it turned out a good plan, you see!" remarked the girl to
the wife. "I knew it would with such as him. He's a dear
good fellow, and you ought to be proud of un."

"I am," said Mrs. Fawley, quietly.

"And when do you expect — ?"

"S-sh! Not at all."

"What!"

"I was mistaken."

"Ah, Arabella, Arabella; you be a deep one! Mistaken! Well, that's clever — it's a rale stroke of genius! It's a thing I never thought o', wi' all my experience! I never thought beyond the rale thing — not that one could sham it!"

"Don't you be too quick to cry sham! 'Twasn't sham. I didn't know."

"My word — won't he be in a taking! He'll give it to 'ee o' Saturday nights! Whatever it was, he'll say it was a trick — a double one, by the Lord!"

"I'll own to the first, but not to the second . . . Pooh — he won't care! He'll be glad I was wrong in what I said. He'll shake down, bless 'ee — men always do. What can 'em do otherwise? Married is married." [13]

Now in the serial this conversation is abridged and modified to read thus:

As usual, they laughed before talking; the world seemed funny to them without saying it. "So it turned out a good plan, you see!" remarked the girl to the wife. "I knew it would with such as him. He's a dear good fellow, and you ought to be proud of un."

"I be," said Mrs. Fawley quietly.

"And when be you going to tell him there was no other young man in the case?"

"S-sh! Not at all."

"Afraid to? You think he'll be in a taking, and give it to 'ee o' Saturday nights."

"Pooh — he won't care. I'd own to it for that matter. He'll shake down, bless 'ee — men always do. What can 'em do otherwise? Married is married." [14]

Again alterations occur in Arabella's announcement to Jude — in the book that no child is coming, in the serial that the letter from the Aldbrickham lover was a "mistake." Jude and Arabella are in their room when this announcement takes place. He is reproving her for making dimples in her cheeks, and suggests his displeasure over the fact that she has served in an Aldbrickham tap room. She defends herself.

From the book:

"There was not much to do at home, and I was eating my head off, so I went away for three months."

"You'll soon have plenty to do now, dear, won't you?"

"How do you mean?"

"Why, of course — little things to make."

"Oh!"

"When will it be? Can't you tell me exactly, instead of in such general terms as you have used?"

"Tell you?"

"Yes — the date."

"There's nothing to tell. I made a mistake."

"What?"

"It was a mistake."

He sat bolt upright in bed and looked at her. "How can that be?"

"People fancy wrong things sometimes."

"But — ! Why, of course, so unprepared as I was, without a stick of furniture, and hardly a shilling, I shouldn't have hurried on our affair, and brought you to a half-furnished hut before I was ready, if it had not been for the news you gave me, which made it necessary to save you, ready or no . . . Good God!"

"Don't take on, dear. What's done can't be undone."

"I have no more to say!"

He gave the answer simply, and lay down; and there was silence between them.[15]

From the serial:

"There was not much to do at home, and I was eating my head off, so I went away for three months."

"And then you met with that rival who frightened me lest I should lose you. When are you going to tell me all of that story?"

"Tell you?"

"Yes. Did you ever hear more of him?"

"Oh, there's nothing to tell. I made a mistake."

"What?"

"It was a mistake — about his seriously wanting me."

He sat in bed and looked at her. "How can that be?"

"People fancy wrong things sometimes."

"But —! Why, of course, so unprepared as I was without a stick of furniture, and hardly a shilling — I shouldn't have hurried on our affair, and brought you to a half-furnished hut before I was ready, if it had not been for the news you gave me, which made it imperative for me to declare my intentions. Good God . . . wasn't that story true?"

"Don't take on, dear. What's done can't be undone."

"I have no more to say!"

He gave the answer simply, and lay down; and there was silence.[16]

It is surely unnecessary, in view of the exhaustive

treatment of the preceding incident, to comment upon the absurdity of these alterations! The rest of the narrative concerning the married life of Jude and Arabella is practically the same in book and serial, though there are many minor differences which I have neither time nor space to present here.[17]

An interesting, though perhaps not particularly significant change in the serial version, is seen in the treatment of incident nine — in which Jude writes to five learned Christminster doctors to ask their opinion and advice as to his attempting to enter one of the colleges. The preliminary situation in both book and serial is the same. Jude is attracted by the benign and considerate face of the Head of one of the colleges, and thereupon decides to ask advice. In the book, however, he selects *five* Masters, "whose physiognomies seemed to say to him that they were appreciative and far-seeing men," [18] and whom he has seen during the week following his glimpse of the first, whereas in the serial he writes to but one — that one the Master whose benign face has first attracted him. In the book he receives a reply to but one of his letters; in the serial he receives a reply to the only one written. Although the difference in treatment here is, perhaps, not significant, one can easily see the added irony afforded by the book version. In a minor detail such as this it may be that the change was made in the final revision of the original form when it was prepared for book publication. If the alteration was made from book to serial, it is possible that the editor (or author) wished to avoid in the magazine version the suggestion of intellectual snobbery on the part of the Christminster doctors, just as, in three other instances, he avoided in the magazine certain expressions suggestive of religious satire.[19]

Avoidance of impropriety in the serial version is again shown in the treatment of incident sixteen. Here Jude unexpectedly meets Arabella in a Christminster inn and is induced by her to spend the night in a third-rate hotel in Aldbrickham. The next morning, after they have returned to Christminster (Jude heartily disgusted with himself), they walk a short distance out of the town, and Arabella tells him that she has been legally married in Australia.

Now, in the serial they do not spend the night together. Instead each goes to his own lodging after planning to meet again on the morrow. The next morning they walk a little way out of the town, and on the way Arabella tells Jude of her marriage. It is needless to comment upon the very obvious fact that consistency in the characterization of both Jude and Arabella is again sacrificed for propriety.[20]

The details of incident nineteen, the next incident materially altered for the serial, are not radically different in the book from what they are in the serial. In both, Sue, after leaving Phillotson's room for a bed in the clothes-closet, the night following her farewell to Jude in Marygreen, confesses to Phillotson her aversion to him as a husband; in both she asks his permission to leave him and go to Jude. But there are differ-

ences in the treatment of these details. In the book Sue
is more frank in the expression of her opinions upon
marriage — a frankness which was evidently not
deemed permissible in the serial.   Phillotson, who in
the serial plays the part of a listener to Sue, is in the
book more carefully characterized by his remons-
trances. I quote the passages from both book and
serial in which these differences occur:

From the book:

[Sue is speaking] ". . . Will you let me go away? I
know how irregular it is of me to ask it —"

"It is irregular."

"But I do ask it. Domestic laws should be made according
to temperaments, which should be classified. If people are at
all peculiar in character they have to suffer from the very rules
that produce comfort in others! Will you let me?"

"But we married —"

"What is the use of thinking of laws and ordinances," she
burst out, "if they make you miserable when you know you are
committing no sin?"

"But you are committing a sin in not liking me!"

"I *do* like you! But I didn't reflect it would be — that it
would be so much more than that. . . .   For a man and
woman to live on intimate terms when one feels as I do is adultery, in any circumstances, however legal. There — I've said
it! . . . Will you let me, Richard?"

"You distress me, Susanna, by such importunity!" [21]

From the serial:

"Will you let me go away? I know how irregular it is of
me to ask it."

"It is irregular."

"But domestic laws should be made according to temperaments, which should be classified. If people are at all peculiar in character they have to suffer from the very regulations that produce comfort in others! What is the use of thinking of laws and ordinances if they make you miserable when you know you are committing no sin? There is only one law on this subject in Nature or in God's eye — whichever expression you like best for the same thing — and that is that for a man and woman who don't love each other to live on intimate terms is wrongdoing in any circumstances." [22]

There is a significant alteration, too, in the serial treatment of Sue's plans to go to Jude if Phillotson will release her. In the book, she frankly states that she means "living with Jude." "As his wife?" asks Phillotson. "As I choose," she replies. In the serial this conversation is omitted, and in reply to Phillotson's question, "And do you mean, by living away from me, living by yourself?" she answers: "Well, if you insisted, yes. But I meant living as I choose. Perhaps with my cousin as a companion." By her remark and by the significant omission of Phillotson's question, "As his wife?" and of her reply, we are made to understand that, if she lives with Jude, their relationship is to be conventional enough to suit the most conservative of magazine readers.[23]

A great part of incident twenty-one — that dealing with Sue's departure from Phillotson and her meeting with Jude, who takes her to Aldbrickham — is entirely omitted from the serial. To give exactly the material omitted would mean the quoting of nearly eight pages, a procedure alike unnecessary and inadvisable in a chapter already assuming unanticipated proportions. I shall, therefore, give an adequate summary of it:

Jude, who gets into Sue's compartment at Melchester, tells her that they are booked for Aldbrickham and that he has wired for a room for them at the Temperance Hotel there. Sue, distressed at the announcement that he has asked for but one room, confesses to him that she does not mean to live in intimate relations with him. Surprised as Jude is, he promises to comply with her wishes, and they go on to Aldbrickham. Once there Sue refuses to go to the Temperance Hotel because of the form of his telegram, and they inquire for another, which upon their arrival proves to be the very one at which Jude had stayed over night with Arabella. He does not recognize it at first, but the waitress in his absence tells Sue that she remembers Jude's coming with another woman. Sue, distressed and jealous, upbraids Jude upon his return. He tries to explain his conduct with Arabella, but she is unable to understand it, since at that very time he had said he cared for nobody but her. He explains to her his ignorance of Arabella's marriage at the time, and she becomes less reproachful. They part for the night, he assuring her that he is comparatively happy just to be near her.

None of this material is in the serial. That account, after narrating Sue's departure from Phillotson almost exactly as it is in the book, tells of her meeting with Jude, and of his announcement that he has engaged a lodging for her in Aldbrickham exactly opposite his own, so that they will be able to talk across the street. But that is all. Again the sensibilities of serial readers were spared, and again the characterization of Jude suffered from lack of consistency.[24]

Incidents twenty-two and twenty-three with their alterations for the serial are best presented together. Briefly, they deal in both book and serial with the Aldbrickham life of Sue and Jude, who, though their respective divorces are granted, do not live together as man and wife; with the coming of Arabella in need of help; and with Sue's objections to Jude's going to the inn to give her that help. But there are significant alterations in the serial version.

First, in the book Jude and Sue live in Jude's house "in precisely the same relations that they had established between themselves when she left Shaston[25] to join him the year before," [26] though "with only a landing between them";[27] in the serial, Sue lives in Jude's house and manages it for him, but he has a room "exactly opposite, the street being so narrow that they could call to each other across it." [28] So careful, indeed, is the serial editor (or author) to "avoid the least appearance of evil" that he will not allow Jude to kiss Sue when he has come across the street to breakfast. Instead, he shakes hands with her! [28]

Secondly, in the book Sue, in order to prevent Jude from going to Arabella, promises to give herself to Jude that night. The conversation between them is perfectly clear in its suggestion:

"I have nobody but you, Jude, and you are deserting me! I didn't know you were like this — I can't bear it, I can't. If she were yours, it would be different!"

"Or if you were."

"Very well, then — if I must, I must. Since you will have it so, I agree! Only I didn't mean to! And I didn't want to marry again either. . . . But yes — I agree! I ought to have known you would conquer in the long-run, living like this!"

She ran across and flung her arms around his neck. "I am not a cold-natured, sexless creature, am I, for keeping you at such a distance? I am sure you don't think so! Wait and see! I do belong to you, don't I? I give in."

"And I'll arrange for our marriage tomorrow, or as soon as ever you wish."

"Yes, Jude."

"Then I'll let her go," said he, embracing Sue softly. . . . "She is not like you, my darling, and never was. . . . Don't cry any more. There, and there, and there!" He kissed her on one side, and on the other, and in the middle, and re-bolted the front door."[29]

Moreover, Sue's conversation with Arabella, whom, in a kind of triumphant pity, she visits the next morning at the inn, confirms the suggestion:

Arabella lay facing the window, and did not at once turn her head. . . . The sight of her own fresh charms in the look-ing-glass made Sue's manner bright, till she reflected what a meanly sexual emotion this was in her, and hated herself for it.

"I've just looked in to see if you got back comfortably last night, that's all," she said gently. . . .

"Oh, how stupid this is! I thought my visitor was — your

friend — your husband — Mrs. Fawley, as I suppose you call yourself?" said Arabella, flinging her head back upon the pillows with a disappointed toss, and ceasing to retain the dimple she had just taken the trouble to produce.

"Indeed I don't," said Sue.

"Oh, I thought you might have, even if he's not legally yours. Decency is decency, any hour of the twenty-four."

"I don't know what you mean," said Sue stiffly. "He is mine, if you come to that!"

"He wasn't yesterday."

Sue colored roseate, and said, "How do you know?"

"From your manner when you talked to me at the door. Well, my dear, you've been quick about it, and I expect my visit last night helped it on — ha-ha! But I don't want to get him away from you." [30]

The corresponding passages in the serial plainly show the difference in treatment.

The first, dealing with the conversation between Jude and Sue:

"I have nobody but you, Jude, and you are deserting me! I didn't know you were like this — I can't bear it. I can't! If she were yours it would be different!"

"Or if you were, dear. Now come; why won't you be? Will you be my wife, and put an end to this state of things? If you'll promise that, I'll stay, and let her go her ways."

"Oh — I, if I must, I must — if you make me! You are the strongest, and I am the weak one!"

"No; I shan't have you on those terms. No compulsion, but voluntarily."

"Very well, then, since you will have it so, I agree! Only I didn't mean to marry again! But yes — I agree, I agree!

I ought to have known that you would conquer in the long-run, living like this!"

She ran across and flung her arms round his neck. "I am not a cold-natured, heartless creature, am I, for keeping you at such a distance? I am sure you don't think so! Wait and see! I do belong to you, don't I? I give in about my arguments! You can arrange for our marriage to-morrow, or as soon as ever you wish."

"Then I'll let her go," said he, embracing Sue softly. . . . "She is not like you, my darling, and never was. . . . Don't cry any more. There, and there, and there!" He kissed her on one side, and on the other, and in the middle, and waiting till the street was empty, slipped across the way to his room.[31]

The second, the conversation between Arabella and Sue:

Arabella lay facing the window, and did not at once turn her head. . . . The sight of her own fresh charms in the looking-glass made Sue's manner bright, till she reflected what a meanly sexual emotion this was in her, and hated herself for it.

"I've just looked in to see if you got back comfortably last night, that's all," she said gently. . . .

"Oh, how stupid this is! I thought my visitor was — your friend — your husband — Mrs. Fawley, as I suppose you call yourself?" said Arabella, flinging her head back upon the pillows with a disappointed toss, and ceasing to retain the dimple she had just taken the trouble to produce.

"Indeed I don't," said Sue.

"Oh, I thought you might have, even if he's not legally yours. Decency is decency, any hour of the day."

"I — don't know what you mean," said Sue, stiffly. "He is

mine in promise if you come to that! We have fixed the day and everything!"

"It wasn't fixed yesterday."

Sue colored scarlet, and said, "How do you know?"

"From your manner when you talked to me at the door. Well, my dear, you've been quick about it, and I expect my visit last night helped it on — ha-ha! But I don't want to get him away from you." [32]

The avoidance in the serial of the establishment of intimacy between Sue and Jude just when it would most naturally take place (*i.e.* upon the ominous reappearance of Arabella), and the substitution of Sue's promise to marry Jude on the morrow, should certainly, at least in the consequences, have tested the credulity of even the most cursory serial reader. For, one naturally asks, what does Jude gain, since in the morning Sue decides that she is afraid to marry on account of the ill resulting from other marriages in their family? Since he has given up going to Arabella solely because of Sue's promise to marry him, is it consistent, or natural, for him on the following day to acquiesce readily in Sue's desire to turn away from the house of the parish-clerk, and to come willingly back to live in his room across the street? And, pray, what does the author mean to suggest when he announces in the serial, just as in the book, that, after they postponed their marriage, they "seemed to live on in a dreamy paradise?" [33] Why more of a paradise than before when affairs between them remained the same — when they were living as before — "on the same friendly footing"?

Could there be a greater sacrifice of plausibility than is brought about by the suppression of consistent material and this substitution of the incredible? And if substitutions and omissions had to be made, one is tempted to ask why they could not have been done more carefully and thoroughly, so that at least the term "dreamy paradise" might not characterize the life of a pair of lovers who have decided to give up the marriage they agreed upon, and who still live apart?

It is impossible to catalogue here the many minor alterations made in the serial version of incident twenty-six — the second unsuccessful attempt of Sue and Jude to marry, the speculation of their neighbors upon their relations and upon the identity of the child, and, finally, the social ostracism accorded them when their first child is about to come. There are no extensive omissions from the serial, but there are numerous changes in it made necessary by the facts that Sue and Jude, in the minds of serial readers, still live apart, and that of course she is to have no child. Two slight omissions occur in the magazine story, however, which I think are worth mention: first, the paragraphs having to do with a trip away taken by Jude and Sue, with the view of persuading people that they have been married at last; and second, a conversation between them as they work together in redecorating the Ten Commandments in a country church, and after they have overheard certain remarks concerning them made by those connected with the church. I quote these omitted passages:

The result was that shortly after the attempt at the registrar's the pair went off — to London it was believed — for
several days, hiring somebody to look to the boy. When they
came back they let it be understood indirectly, and with total
indifference and weariness of mien, that they were legally married at last. Sue, who had previously been called Mrs. Bridehead, now openly adopted the name of Mrs. Fawley. Her dull,
cowed, and listless manner for days seemed to substantiate all
this.

But the mistake (as it was called) of their going away so
secretly to do the business kept up much of the mystery of their
lives; and they found that they not made such advances with
their neighbors as they had expected to do thereby. A living
mystery was not much less interesting than a dead scandal.[34]

Certain persons connected with the church are questioning among themselves whether or not Sue is married to Jude:

"Some say Yes; some say No" . .

"Not? Then she ought to be, or somebody's — that's very
clear!"

"They've only been married a few weeks, whether or no."

. . . .

However, in a few minutes Sue seemed to see that their
position this morning had a ludicrous side, and, wiping her
eyes, she laughed.

"It is droll, after all," she said, "that we two, of all people,
with our queer history, should happen to be here doing this!
You a reprobate, and I — in my condition. . . . Oh,
dear!" And with her hand over her eyes she laughed again
silently and intermittently, till she was quite weak.

"That's better," said Jude gayly. "Now we are right again,
aren't we, little girl?"

"Oh, but it is serious, all the same." She sighed, as she took up the brush and righted herself. "But do you see they don't think we are married? They won't believe it! It is extraordinary!"

"I don't care whether they think so or not," said Jude. "I shan't take any more trouble to make them." [35]

An interesting alteration in the serial version of the story occurs in the treatment of incident twenty-eight. Here Sue, after nearly two years of moving with Jude from place to place, is discovered at Kennetbridge fair by Arabella, who has, since the death of her husband, become a chapel-goer. Sue is selling gingerbread cakes, which Jude, who has been too ill to work at his trade, has modelled after the towers and pinnacles of Christminster. The major details in book and serial are identical, but necessary changes are made in the latter, again as always because of the conventional relations still existing in the serial between Sue and Jude. These changes are shown especially in the conversation between Sue and Arabella, who has been boldly questioning Sue concerning the details of her life with Jude and the boy, Arabella's child. I give here the conversations of the book and of the serial.

From the book:

"Then you are living with him still?"
"Yes."
"Married?"
"Of course."
"Any children?"
"Two."

"And another coming soon, I see."

Sue writhed under the hard and direct questioning, and her tender little mouth began to quiver.

"Lord — I mean goodness gracious — what is there to cry about? Some folks would be proud enough!"

"It is not that I am ashamed — not as you think! But it seems such a terribly tragic thing to bring beings into the world — so presumptuous — that I question my right to do it sometimes!"

"Take it easy, my dear. . . . But you don't tell me why you do such a thing as this? Jude used to be a proud sort of chap — above any business almost, leave alone keeping a standing."

"Perhaps my husband has altered a little since then. I am sure he is not proud now," and Sue's lips quivered again. "I am doing this because he caught a chill early in the year. . . . He is better than he was; but it has been a long, weary time! We have had an old widow friend with us to help us through it; but she's leaving soon." [36]

From the serial:

"Then you did marry?"

"No — I live near him — it is absolutely necessary now."

Sue writhed under the hard and direct questioning, and her tender little mouth began to quiver.

"Lord — I mean goodness — what is there to cry about? Some folks would take it easy enough."

"It is not that I am ashamed of keeping the state — not as you think!"

"But you don't tell me why you do such a thing as this? Jude used to be a proud sort of chap — above any business almost, leave alone keeping a standing."

"Perhaps he has altered a little. I am sure he is not proud

now." And Sue's lips quivered again. "I am doing this because he caught a chill early in the year. . . . He is better than he was, but it has been a long, weary time! He has an old widow friend from Marygreen to nurse him, for I have enough to do with teaching his boy, and another little child I have adopted, whose parents died and left him at the mercy of the world."

"Well — well — to think you didn't marry after all!"

"Fortunately for us, we didn't. Jude might have felt hampered now if he had married me; while I can act for him now of my own free will." [37]

As the plot of the serial proceeds, it becomes more impossible. Three more years of living together and yet apart, and an *adopted* child!

There is one significant omission in the serial treatment of incident thirty-one, the details of which in the book are as follows: Jude and Sue, with Jude's boy and their own two children (in the serial, Jude's child and the one adopted by Sue), return to Christminster. There they find it difficult to get lodgings on account of the children, and of Sue's approaching confinement; and their own discouragement affects the boy — strangely old and reflective for his years. Sue, alone with him in temporary lodgings from which, they have learned, they must go in the morning, tells him, to conclude a conversation they have had concerning the injustice of bringing children into the world, that another child is coming. Now in the serial she *does* hold the conversation with him, but she does not, of course, tell him of the coming of the other baby. The following conversation is, then, omitted, and the serial thus loses one of the most tragic and dramatic scenes of the novel:

She at last concluded that, so far as circumstances permitted, she would be honest and candid with one who entered into her difficulties like an aged friend.

"There is going to be another in our family soon," she hesitatingly remarked.

"How?"

"There is going to be another baby."

"What!" The boy jumped up wildly. "O God, mother, you've never a-sent for another; and such trouble with what you've got!"

"Yes, I have, I am sorry to say," murmured Sue, her eyes glistening with suspended tears.

The boy burst out weeping. "Oh, you don't care, you don't care!" he cried in bitter reproach. "How *ever* could you, mother, be so wicked and cruel as this, when you needn't have done it till we was better off, and father well! To bring us all into *more* trouble! No room for us, and father a-forced to go away, and we turned out tomorrow; and yet you be going to have another of us soon! . . . 'Tis done o' purpose — 'tis — 'tis!" He walked up and down sobbing.

"You must forgive me, little Jude!" she pleaded, her bosom heaving now as much as the boy's. "I can't explain; I will when you are older. It does seem as if I had done it on purpose, now we are in these difficulties. I can't explain, dear. But it — it is not quite on purpose; I can't help it."

"Yes it is — it must be! For nobody would interfere with us, like that, unless you agreed! I won't forgive you, ever, ever! I'll never believe you care for me, or father, or any of us any more!" [38]

The awful catastrophe of the murder of the two younger children by little Jude, and of his suicide, is of course modified somewhat in the serial, since there the children number but two, Jude and the adopted child. The description of the tragedy is, however, practically identical with that in the book, with the exception of the few necessary modifications,[39] and of the following description of little Jude's dead face, a description omitted in the serial:

The boy's face expressed the whole tale of their situation. On that little shape had converged all the inauspiciousness and shadow which had darkened the first union of Jude, and all the accidents, mistakes, fears, errors of the last. He was their nodal point, their focus, their expression in a single term. For the rashness of those parents he had groaned, for their ill-assortment he had quaked, and for the misfortunes of these he had died.[40]

The serial necessarily presents less motivation for the tragedy since it lacks Sue's confidence to the boy, which is in the book the culminating motivation.

Incident thirty-three is, in its entirety, absent from the serial version of the novel. Quotation of it from the book is, I think, unnecessary. I therefore give a brief summary:

After Jude has seen the children buried, he hurries back to Sue, who is sleeping. He returns again to her later, and finds her gone. Alarmed, he goes again to the cemetery where he finds her expostulating with a man who is earthing in the children's graves, and begging him to let her see them once more. Jude finally persuades her to leave the cemetery with him. That night she gives birth to a still-born child.[41]

The culmination of the life of Sue and Jude as man and wife comes in incident thirty-five. It is motivated by Sue's return to an interest in the Church, by her growing belief in self-renunciation, and finally by her conviction that she is still the wife of Richard Phillotson in the sight of Heaven, and must not continue to live with Jude. She, therefore, in a tremendously dramatic scene, tells him that she cannot live with him any longer, and sends him from her.

Now, in the serial account of this incident the motivation is necessarily weaker. Sue's interest in the Church is the same, as is her conviction that she is still the wife of Phillotson in the sight of Heaven. The weakness in the motivation is, then, in her idea of self-renunciation, for obviously she has far less to renounce in the serial, since she and Jude have not lived together. Jude has, to be sure, here as in the book, planned to marry as soon as she is able to go out, though, since Sue has never acquiesced in the plan, one can hardly feel that she is *renouncing* marriage with him.

The alterations in this renunciatory scene made for the serial are, therefore, particularly interesting, and show, as well as any incident thus far presented, the great sacrifice of verisimilitude in plot. I am quoting, with several abridgments, the scene from the book and then from the serial.

Jude has found Sue late one night in St. Silas' church, and is taking her home:

They went on till they came to a little coffee-house. "Jude," she said, with suppressed tears, "would you mind getting a lodging here?"

"I will — if, if you really wish? But do you? Let me go to our door, and understand you."

He went and conducted her in. She said she wanted no supper, and went in the dark up-stairs and struck a light. Turning she found that Jude had followed her, and was standing at the chamber door. She went to him, put her hand in his, and said, "Good-night."

"But, Sue! Don't we live here?"

"You said you would do as I wished!"

"Yes. Very well! . . . Perhaps it was wrong of me to argue distastefully as I have done! Perhaps, as we couldn't conscientiously marry at first in the old-fashioned way, we ought to have parted. Perhaps the world is not illuminated enough for such experiments as ours! Who were we, to think we could act as pioneers!"

"I am so glad you see that much, at any rate. I never deliberately meant to do as I did. I slipped into my false position through jealousy and agitation."

"But surely through love — you loved me?"

"Yes. But I wanted to let it stop there and go on always as mere lovers; until —"

"But people in love couldn't live forever like that!"

"Women could; men can't because they — won't. An average woman is in this superior to an average man — that she never instigates, only responds. We ought to have lived in mental communion, and no more."

"I was the unhappy cause of the change, as I have said before. . . . Well, as you will. . . . But human nature can't help being itself."

"Oh yes — that's just what it has to learn — self-mastery."

"I repeat — if either were to blame it was not you, but I."

"No — it was I. Your wickedness was only the natural man's desire to possess the woman. Mine was not the reciprocal wish till envy stimulated me to oust Arabella. I had thought I ought in charity to let you approach me — that it was damnably selfish to torture you as I did my other friend. But I shouldn't have given way if you hadn't broken me down by making me fear you would go back to her. . . . But don't let us say any more about it. Jude, will you leave me to myself now?"

"Yes. . . . But Sue — my wife, as you are!" he burst out — "my old reproach to you was, after all, a true one. You have never loved me as I love you — never — never! . . . And now you add to your cruelty by leaving me!"

"Ah — yes! The further I flounder, the more harm I do!"

"Oh, Sue!" said he, with a sudden sense of his own danger. "Do not do an immoral thing for moral reasons. You have been my social salvation. Stay with me for humanity's sake! You know what a weak fellow I am. My two Arch Enemies you know — my weakness for women and my impulse to strong liquor. Don't abandon me to them, Sue, . . . Since I have had you I have been able to go into any temptations of the sort without risk. Isn't my safety worth a little sacrifice of dogmatic principle? I am in terror lest, if you leave me, it will be with me another case of the pig that was washed turning back to his wallowing in the mire!"

Sue burst out weeping. "Oh, but you must not, Jude! You won't! I'll pray for you night and day!"

"Well, never mind; don't grieve," said Jude, generously. "I did suffer, God knows, about you at that time; and now I suffer again. But perhaps not so much as you. The woman mostly gets the worst of it in the long-run."

"She does."

"Unless she is absolutely worthless and contemptible! And this one is not that anyhow!"

Sue drew a nervous breath or two. "She is — I fear. . . . Now, Jude — good-night — please!"

"I mustn't stay? Not just once more? As it has been so many times. Oh, Sue, my wife, why not?"

"No — no — not wife! . . . I am in your hands, Jude, don't tempt me back, now I have advanced so far!"

"Very well. I do your bidding. I owe that to you, darling, in penance for how I overruled it at the first time. My God, how selfish I was! Perhaps — perhaps I spoiled one of the highest and purest loves that ever existed between man and woman! . . . Then let the veil of our temple be rent in two from this hour!"

He went to the bed, removed one of the pillows thereon, and flung it to the floor.

Sue looked at him, and bending over the bed-rail, wept silently. "You don't see that it is a matter of conscience with me, and not of dislike to you!" she brokenly murmured. . . . But I can't say any more — it breaks my heart — it will be undoing all I have begun, Jude — good-night!"

"Good-night," he said, and turned to go.

"Oh, but you shall kiss me!" said she. . . . "I can't bear . . ."

He clasped her, and kissed her weeping face as he had scarcely ever done before, and they remained in silence till she said, "Good-bye, good-bye!" And then gently pressing him away she got free, trying to mitigate the sadness by saying: "We'll be dear friends just the same, Jude, won't we? And we'll see each other sometimes — yes! and forget all this, and try to be as we were long ago?"

Jude did not permit himself to speak, but turned and descended the stairs.[42]

From the serial:

They went on. "Jude," she said, "would you mind going home now?"

"I'll do what you wish. But let me go to your door."

He went. She put her hand in his, and said, "Good-night."

"But Sue!" He had bent his face to hers.

"You said you would do as I wished!"

"Yes. Very well. . . . Perhaps it was wrong of me to argue as I have done! If you can't conscientiously marry again, I cannot make you."

"I am so glad you see that much, at any rate."

"But surely you love — you have loved me?"

"Yes. But I want to let it stop here."

"But people in love can't go on forever like this!"

"Women could; men can't, because they — won't. An average woman is in this superior to man."

"As you will. But human nature can't help being itself."

"Oh yes — that's just what it has to learn — self-mastery."

"Well — if either were to blame for our unconventional doings it was not you, but I."

"Don't let us say any more about it, Jude, will you leave me to myself now?"

"Yes. . . . But Sue!" he burst out — "my old reproach to you was, after all, a true one. You have never loved me as I love you — never — never! . . . And now you add to your cruelty by leaving me without hope."

"Ah — yes! The further I flounder, the more harm I do!"

"Well, never mind; don't grieve," said Jude, generously. "I did suffer, God knows, about you at that time; and now I suffer again. But perhaps not so much as you. The woman mostly gets the worst of it in the long-run."

"She does."

"Unless she is absolutely worthless and contemptible! And you are not that anyhow!"

Sue drew a nervous breath or two. "Now, Jude — good-night — please!"

"Good-night! . . . Then the veil of our temple is to be rent from this hour?"

She looked at him, and wept silently. "You don't see that it is a matter of conscience with me, and not of dislike to you!" she brokenly murmured. "Dislike to you! But I can't say any more — it breaks my heart — it will be undoing all I have begun!"

"Very well," he said, and turned to go.

"Oh, but you shall kiss me!" said she. "I can't bear —"

He clasped her, and kissed her weeping face as he had scarcely ever done before, and they remained in silence, till she said, "Good-bye; good-bye!" And then gently pressing him away, she got free, trying to mitigate the sadness by saying: "We'll be dear friends just the same, Jude, won't we? And we'll see each other sometimes — yes! — and forget all this, and try to be as we were long ago?"

Jude did not permit himself to speak, but turned and went along the street.[43]

There is one significant difference between the book and the serial version of incident thirty-five — the decision of Phillotson to ask Sue to come back to him — and that difference lies in Phillotson's reason for so doing. In the book we are told plainly that his reason "had at bottom nothing to do with repentance of letting her go, but was, primarily, a human instinct flying in the face of custom and profession." [44]   Again, we read that "he wished for her still, in his curious way, if he did not love her, and, apart from policy, soon felt that he would be gratified to have her again as his, always provided that she came willingly." [45]   Finally we learn that since "artifice was necessary . . . for stemming the cold and inhumane blast of the world's contempt, . . . here were the materials ready made. By getting Sue back and re-marrying her on the respectable plea of having entertained erroneous views of her, and gained his divorce wrongfully, he might acquire some comfort, resume his old courses, perhaps return to the Shaston school if not even to the Church itself as a licentiate." [46]

In the serial, on the other hand, Phillotson is not a prey to human instincts. (As we have already discovered, the serial avoids human instincts!) He has suffered actual privations in sticking to his convictions of right and justice and allowing Sue to leave him — so much so, indeed, that his convictions have been "nearly thrashed out of him." [47]   Now he wants comfort and reinstatement in the eyes of the world, and he thinks that by asking Sue back and remarrying her, he may respectably regain these desired ends. In other words, policy, pure and simple, dictates his invitation to her — the policy which, in the book, is "artifice" used to conceal his desire for her.

In the details of Sue's return and remarriage to him there are many minor alterations in the serial,[48] but none worthy of much space. It is interesting to note, however, that in the book, after the marriage, Phillotson, who has to his dismay found that Sue's aversion to him has not changed, says to her:

"Of course, my dear, I shan't expect to intrude upon your personal privacy any more than I did before. . . . It is for our good socially to do this, and that's its justification, if it was not my reason." [49]

In the serial he makes no such remark, and we have no reason to believe that Sue did not at once assume the full responsibilities of marriage with him.

The story of Arabella's search for Jude, her discovery of him the day after Sue's remarriage with Phillotson, her forcing of herself upon him on the plea that she is penniless, and, finally, her taking him home, drunk, to her father's house — happenings all of which culminate a few days later in his marrying her again — has one significant difference in the serial. For even Arabella, though she may force herself upon Jude, though she may, indeed, make him completely drunk, must draw the line somewhere, at least in the minds of serial readers, inconsistent as she may become by so doing. Consequently, although in the book we are made clearly to understand that Arabella takes Jude home and to her own room for the night, and that, in the words of her father, they "have been living together these three or four days" [50] before the marriage takes place, in the serial all such unconventionalities are carefully avoided. Arabella takes Jude home, to be sure — they are both drunk in the serial as well as in the book

— but we are spared the details of their ascending the stairs to Arabella's room, and are hastily assured that Jude is "in the spare room." [51]

Incidents thirty-nine and forty, with the accompanying alterations and omissions in the serial, are best treated together. They deal, first, with the pathetic journey of Jude to Marygreen to see Sue once more; second, with the tensely dramatic scene with Sue in the church; and third, with Sue's self-imposed penance thereafter.

Jude's journey to Marygreen and his anonymous message to Sue to meet him in the church are practically identical in book and serial.

The scene between Sue and Jude in the church presents significant alterations. From one of the most dramatic scenes in the novel it is cut down and altered until it loses practically all its intensity. In the serial Sue is almost angry with Jude, she reiterates her belief in Phillotson as her husband "ordained of heaven," she begs Jude not to awake in her any feelings of love for him, and finally, upon his suggestion that they go away together (a suggestion entirely unmotivated in the serial, for Sue has shown him no mark of affection), she begs him to leave her and he does so.

What a satisfying difference in the book! Here Sue and Jude are both entirely consistent, and here Jude's suggestion that they go away together is adequately motivated. Their last meeting is, therefore, perfectly satisfactory from the point of view of consistency and of plausibility.

The following passage, entirely omitted from the serial, illustrates the points of superiority enumerated above. Sue has just told Jude for the first time to leave her. He speaks:

"I will. I would never come to see you again, even if I had the strength to come, which I shall not have any more. Sue, Sue, you are not worth a man's love!"

Her bosom began to go up and down. "I can't endure you to say that!" she burst out; and her eye resting on him a moment, she turned back impulsively. "Don't, don't scorn me! Kiss me — oh, kiss me! — lots of times, and say I am not a coward and a contemptible humbug — I can't bear it!" She rushed up to him, and, with her mouth on his, continued: "I must tell you — oh, I must — my darling love! It has been only a church marriage — an apparent marriage, I mean! He suggested it at the very first!"

"How?"

"I mean it is a nominal marriage only. It hasn't been more than that at all since I came back to him!"

"Sue!" he said. Pressing her to him in his arms, he bruised her lips with kisses. "If misery can know happiness, I have a moment's happiness now! Now, in the name of all you hold holy, tell me the truth and no lie. You do love me still?"

"I do! You know it too well! . . . But I *mustn't* do this! I mustn't kiss you back as I would!"

"But do!"

"And yet you are so dear! — and you look so ill —"

"And so do you! There's one more, in memory of our dead little children — yours and mine!"

The words struck her like a blow, and she bent her head. "I *mustn't* — I *can't* go on with this!" she gasped presently. "But there, there, darling, I give you back your kisses; I do;

I do! . . . And now I'll hate myself forever for my sin!" [52]

Sue's self-imposed penance — her going that night to Phillotson's room and begging him to take her as his wife, after her oath upon the New Testament that she will never see Jude again — is entirely omitted from the serial. Obviously it has no place there, for, even though it were not offensive to the taste of magazine readers, there is no motivation for it in the serial scene between Sue and Jude in the church. Moreover, the serial has not suggested that Phillotson and Sue have been living on any other terms. It is, of course, needless to comment on the fact that by the omission the serial loses another of the most dramatic and tragic incidents of the novel. [53]

The meeting between Sue and Jude in Marygreen church is, in the serial, the last we see or hear of Sue. In the next to the last chapter of the book, however, Mrs. Edlin comes to see Jude, who is dying at Christminster, and tells him of Sue's penance. Her story incites Jude to bitter expressions of his grief over Sue and of his opinion as to certain social conventions. During Mrs. Edlin's visit the physician Vilbert enters, but Jude hurls such language at him that he leaves precipitately. He, however, meets Arabella in the hall, whereupon she offers him a drink. The quoted passage tells the rest of the story:

She brought him a bottle and a glass, and he drank. Arabella began shaking with suppressed laughter. "What is this, my dear?" he asked, smacking his lips.

"Oh, a drop of wine — and something in it." Laughing again, she said: "I poured your own love-philter into it, that you sold me at the Agricultural Show, don't you remember?"

"I do, I do! Clever woman! But you must be prepared for the consequences." Putting his arm round her shoulders, he kissed her there and then.

"Don't, don't," she whispered, laughing good-humoredly. "My man will hear."

She let him out of the house, and as she went back she said to herself, "Well, weak women must provide for a rainy day. And if my poor fellow up-stairs do go off — as I suppose he will soon — it's well to keep chances open. And I can't pick and choose now as I could when I was younger. And one must take the old if one can't get the young." [54]

All of these details of incidents forty-one and forty-two are omitted, at great sacrifice, from the serial. [55]

The last chapter, which deals with the death of Jude, is altered little in serial version. Three omissions, however, should be noted. It will be remembered that Jude lies dying alone. Arabella cannot resist going to witness the Remembrance Week festivities, and, returning to find him dead, leaves him again to watch the boat-racing.

The first of the three omissions in the serial is the passage which gives the Scriptural verses repeated by Jude in his last moments. There seems to be no adequate reason why this should be omitted from the magazine. Against it, to be sure, might have been urged the charge of blasphemy by devout and literal Christians, but surely there are too many passages in the serial open to just such a charge. Jude in many of his

utterances is blasphemous in the extreme. Why then
should objections be made to these last words of his?
It seems probable to me that, not present in the first
form of the story, the passage was very effectively inserted, for the sake of irony, in the final revision of
that form for book publication. I quote the portion
omitted from the serial:

While he remained, his face changing, shouts and hurrahs
came from somewhere in the direction of the river.

"Ah — yes! The Remembrance games," he murmured.
"And I here. And Sue defiled!"

The hurrahs were repeated, drowning the faint organ notes.
Jude's face changed more; he whispered, slowly, his lips scarcely
moving:

*"Let the day perish wherein I was born, and the night in
which it was said, 'There is a man child conceived.'"*

"Hurrah!"

*"Let that day be darkness; let not God regard it from above,
neither let the light shine upon it. Lo, let that night be solitary, let no joyful voice come therein."*

"Hurrah!"

*"Why died I not from the womb? Why did I not give up
the ghost when I came out of the belly? . . . For now
should I have lain still and been quiet. I should have slept;
then had I been at rest!"*

"Hurrah!"

*"There the prisoners rest together; they hear not the voice of
the oppressor. . . . The small and the great are there;
and the servant is free from his master. Wherefore is light
given to him that is in misery, and life unto the bitter in
soul?"* [56]

The second omission is that of the passages dealing with Arabella and Vilbert. Arabella is approached by the physician as she watches the races, and informed that the love philter is operating, but to her credit be it said that she refuses to talk of love to him on that day. No mention of Vilbert occurs in the serial treatment of this last chapter.[57]

Finally, the end of the novel in the serial is different from that in the book. In the former the story closes with the Widow Edlin and Arabella on either side of Jude's bed, with the voices of the doctors coming into the room from the open windows of the theater, and at the very end with the joyous sound of the college bells. In the book, however, the following passage is added, the effectiveness of which need hardly be commented upon:

Arabella's eyes removed from Jude to Mrs. Edlin. "D'ye think she will come?" she asked.

"I could not say. She swore not to see him again."

"How is she looking?"

"Tired and miserable, poor heart. Years and years older than when you saw her last. Quite a staid, worn woman now. 'Tis the man — she can't stomach un, even now!"

"If Jude had been alive to see her, he would hardly have cared for her any more, perhaps."

"That's what we don't know. . . . Didn't he ever ask you to send for her, since he came to see her in that strange way?"

"No. Quite the contrary. I offered to send, and he said I was not to let her know how ill he was."

"Did he forgive her?"

"Not as I know."

"Well — poor little thing, 'tis to be believed she's found forgiveness somewhere! She said she had found peace!"

"She may swear that on her knees to the holy cross upon her necklace till she's hoarse, but it won't be true," said Arabella. "She's never found peace since she left his arms, and never will again till she's as he is now!" [58]

Since, in the presentation of these various changes in the incidents of the novel, I have repeatedly commented on the great sacrifice of plausibility and consistency for the sake of propriety, in the serial version, reiteration seems hardly necessary.[59] Suffice it to say that *Jude the Obscure* in the serial version surely does not fulfill the definition of it given in the preface of the first edition: ". . . a novel addressed by a man to men and women of full age, which attempts to deal unaffectedly with the fret and fever, derision and disaster, that may press in the wake of the strongest passion known to humanity, and to point, without a mincing of words, the tragedy of unfulfilled aims."

OTHER MINOR CHANGES

Aside from these far-reaching changes in incident and plot made in the serial version of *Jude the Obscure,* there are relatively few other alterations made either from book to serial or — in the case of minor improvements — from the first form to the final one. The characterization, with possibly one slight exception, remains the same in both versions, except of course for the glaring inconsistency in the serial version brought

about by the alterations in incident and plot; there are
practically no improvements in setting; there are few
additions made to enhance the literary atmosphere;
and although there are changes in diction and some
few in sentence structure, they are noticeably fewer in
number than in the other novels studied. I am, therefore, dealing with these few differences in one section,
instead of treating each separately as I have done in
the discussions of *The Mayor of Casterbridge* and
Tess of the D'Urbervilles.

As to differences in characterization made deliberately by the author, there is, as I have said, only one,
and that is more in the nature of an addition than a
difference. In the book Hardy, in three passages absent from the serial, adds to the character of Sue:
First, he emphasizes her impulsive nature;[60] second, he
speaks of her "putting on flippancy to hide real feelings, a common trick with her"; [61] and third, he emphasizes the fact that her nature is a "curious double"
one.[62] In these ways he has impressed Sue upon his
readers, though he has not in any way altered one's
conception of her.

The Wessex setting, which, we discovered, was so
greatly enhanced in the Wessex Novels edition of *The
Mayor* and of *Tess,* needs no emphasis in *Jude.* The
word "Wessex" itself is used again and again, in the
serial as well as in the book; towns are located in
North, East, South, Outer, and Upper Wessex; the
Wessex dialect is several times mentioned, and it is
consistently used as the speech of the uneducated; Wes-

sex weather[63] and Wessex scenery[64] are described. Evidently Hardy meant from the very first to emphasize the Wessex atmosphere of this novel. Thus, by its consistent Wessex atmosphere, does *Jude the Obscure,* the first edition of which came out in the Wessex Novels edition in 1896, add proof to the assumption advanced and, I think, satisfactorily proved, in the discussion of Wessex setting in *The Mayor* and *Tess, i.e.* that the proposed title of the new edition instigated certain changes and additions in the setting of the novels, by which the locality of Wessex might be more prominently featured.

As for additions which enhance the literary tone of the book in contrast with the serial, they are few and brief compared to those in *The Mayor* and in *Tess.* They are, in fact, five in number, and, with the exception of a one-sentence description of Christminster,[65] consist in the addition of certain literary names or of a quotation to the conversation of Jude and Sue.[66]

The improvement in the diction and in the sentence structure of the book in comparison with those of the serial is very evident, though the instances are far fewer than in either of the other novels treated in this study. There are, to be exact, 133 instances of one word or phrase substituted for another for the sake of more exact diction, as against 177 in *The Mayor* and approximately 300 in *Tess.* Of sentences revised for greater clearness there are four as compared with ten in *Tess.* I am referring in a note to the sentences which are improved,[67] and quoting below but three examples of improvements in diction, examples which may fairly be termed typical. The words used in the serial are placed in brackets:

(1) "The spirit of Sue seemed to hover round him and prevent his *flirting and drinking with* [talking to] the frolicsome girls." [68]

(2) "Phillotson trembled, and his naturally pale face *acquired a corpse-like sharpness* [grew sharp] in its lines." [69]

(3) "And they left the tent together, this pot-bellied man and florid woman, in the antipathetic [mutually bored] recriminatory mood of the *average* [typical] husband and wife of Christendom." [70]

NOTES

[1] The other first editions of the Wessex Novels editions are: *The Well-Beloved*, 1897; *Wessex Poems*, 1898; *Poems of the Past and the Present*, 1902; and *A Changed Man*, 1913. (A. P. Webb, *A Bibliography of the Works of Thomas Hardy* (London, 1916), p. 73.)

[2] The first title of the serial story, which ran in *Harper's New Monthly Magazine* from December, 1894, to November, 1895, was *The Simpletons*. It was changed in the January number to *Hearts Insurgent*.

[3] See pp. 52-53 of the annotated book in the University of Minnesota library.

[4] *Ibid.*

[5] See pp. 55-57 of standard Harper edition, or of the annotated copy.

[6] See *Harper's Magazine*, vol. 90, p. 193; or the annotated book, pp. 55-57.

[7] See pp. 59-60 of Harper edition.

[8] See *Harper's Magazine*, vol. 90, p. 194; or the annotated book, p. 59.

[9] See p. 61 in Harper edition.

[10] Sue's characterization of Arabella; see p. 312 in Harper edition.

[11] *Ibid.*, p. 62.

[12] *Ibid.*

[13] See pp. 64-65 in Harper edition.

[14] See pp. 64-65 in annotated book.

[15] See pp. 66-67 in Harper edition.

[16] See pp. 66-67 of the annotated book.

[17] These differences may easily be discovered in chapters x and xi of the annotated book.

[18] See p. 132 of the Harper edition.

[19] For exact details of the difference in the treatment of this incident between the book and the serial, see p. 132 of the annotated book; for the "certain expressions" omitted see pp. 258, 379, 395.

[20] For full understanding of the alterations made in the treatment of this incident, see pp. 216-218 of the annotated book. It is interesting to note on p. 217 an apparent carelessness on the part of Hardy in his revision for the serial. In lines 22-24 he evidently forgets for the moment the serial relations of Jude and Arabella, and allows Jude to say, as he does in the book, "But . . . when we were getting up this morning."

[21] See pp. 263-264, Harper edition.

[22] See pp. 263-264 of the annotated book.

[23] For an understanding of all the alterations made in the serial treatment of this portion of the incident, see pp. 264-265 of the annotated book.

[24] For all of this material, given in the book, but omitted in the serial, see Harper edition, pp. 283-290; for the incident as treated in both, see the same pages of the annotated book.

[25] The home of Phillotson.

[26] See p. 303 in Harper edition.

[27] *Ibid.*, p. 308.

[28] See p. 303 of the annotated book.

[29] See pp. 314-315, in Harper edition.

[30] *Ibid.*, p. 317.

[31] See pp. 314-315 of the annotated book.

[32] *Ibid.*, pp. 316-317.

[33] See p. 322 in Harper edition.

[34] *Ibid.*, pp. 352-353.

[35] *Ibid.*, pp. 358-359.

[36] *Ibid.*, pp. 368-369.

[37] See pp. 368-369 of the annotated book.

[38] See pp. 396-397 in Harper edition.

39 For these modifications see pp. 398-399-400 of the annotated book.

40 See p. 400 in Harper edition.

41 For this incident in full, see pp. 404-406 in Harper edition.

42 *Ibid.*, pp. 419-422.

43 See pp. 419-422 of the annotated book.

44 See p. 436 in Harper edition.

45 *Ibid.*, p. 426.

46 *Ibid.*

47 *Harper's New Monthly Magazine*, vol. 91, p. 756.

48 See pp. 432-441 of the annotated book.

49 *Ibid.*; p. 441 in Harper edition.

50 See p. 455 in Harper edition.

51 See p. 450 of the annotated book. For other serial alterations of this incident see pp. 445-458 of the same book.

52 See pp. 464-465 in Harper edition.

53 For this incident, which is too long to quote, see pp. 469-475 in Harper edition.

54 See p. 479 in Harper edition.

55 For the full text of these omissions, and for all alterations which cannot be quoted here, see pp. 477-479 of the annotated book.

56 See p. 482 in Harper edition.

57 *Ibid.*, pp. 484-486.

58 *Ibid.*, pp. 487-488.

59 There are numerous minor alterations made in the serial obviously for the sake of sparing the sensibilities of the magazine reader. They are so numerous, in fact, that any attempt to catalogue them has been given up. For some of the most interesting see the annotated book, pp. 38, 41, 52, 63, 73, 140, 162, 164, 170, 171, 248, 251, 256, 292, 298, 319, 368, 369.

60 See p. 154 in Harper edition.

61 *Ibid.*, p. 177.

62 *Ibid.*, p. 247.

63 *Ibid.*, p. 106.

64 *Ibid.*, p. 236.

65 See p. 209 of annotated book.

66 *Ibid.*, pp. 118, 172, 266, 418.

67 *Ibid.*, pp. 30, 73, 98, and 265.

68 *Ibid.*, p. 137.

69 *Ibid.*, p. 192.

70 *Ibid.*, p. 350.

CONCLUSIONS

CONCLUSIONS

THE title of this study suggests two proposals: First, a comparative study of several versions of certain novels, and second, a consideration of the reasons for and the significance of certain important changes made therein. I have, to the best of my ability, accomplished the first, and in so doing I have encroached somewhat upon the premises of the second, for, in many instances, I have thought best to suggest the reasons for certain important changes at the time I have presented the alterations themselves. For example, in my discussion of changes made in setting in *The Mayor of Casterbridge* and in *Tess of the D'Urbervilles*, I made clear my assumption that Hardy deliberately heightened the Wessex atmosphere of those novels in preparation for the Osgood-M'Ilvaine Wessex Novels edition of 1895. Again, I have constantly pointed out that the avoidance in the serials of the unconventional and the illicit in relations between men and women was clearly due to a desire on the part of the periodical editors to keep such material from their readers.

My consideration of the *reasons* for these many changes, then, affords in itself no weighty revelation. They are too obvious, it seems to me, to require pro·

found investigation or detailed discussion. As I see them, they are two in number:

First, the minor alterations — those in characterization, in setting, in the improvement of literary atmosphere and of diction and sentence structure — were made simply because of the author's desire to improve the literary quality of his novel before that novel should be published in book form.

Second, the major alterations (those in incident and plot), which were evidently made either to add sensationalism and suspense to his story or to eliminate the extremely unorthodox, the unconventional, and the improper, were necessitated by the demands of the magazine editor, who had bought Hardy's wares, but who must regard the investment in the light of his reading public.

An interesting light is thrown on the demands of these magazine editors by the examination of the periodicals which published the novels under discussion. If one examines the London *Graphic* for the years 1885 to 1887 (*The Mayor of Casterbridge* ran in the *Graphic* from January to May, 1886) and again for the years 1891 and 1892 (*Tess of the D'Urbervilles* was published July to December, 1891) he will easily discover the sort of material in demand. He will see that the *Graphic* editor of that time featured in a given issue *one* story, and that one usually a serial, occasionally by such men as Walter Besant, Henry James, and Thomas Hardy, but more often by authors of far less repute. These stories were more or less sensational in tone, strictly conventional, and appealed to the heart rather than to the head. Among those in the numbers for 1892 one may read a most sensational production entitled *That Wild Wheel* by Frances Eleanor Trollope, a sister-in-law of Anthony, and another serial, *Wolfenberg* by William Black, a romantic tale centering about a courtship on an ocean liner. The rest of the *Graphic's* pages were filled with notes of the day — especially with much illustrated news of the royal family and its royal visitors, with accounts of house-parties at the home of this and of that peer, and with the latest news of famous prelates. Conservatism and convention were evidently the watchwords of its editor.

The same editorial policy was obviously practiced by the editor of the *Illustrated London News*, in which periodical Hardy's *The Well-Beloved* was published from September to December, 1892. The numbers for 1890 afforded their readers Bret Harte's *The Ward of the Golden Gate*, and, in the Christmas number, a tale entitled *Only a Shadow* by Christie Murray and Henry Herman. Since the last-named story is so typical of the sort of fiction evidently in demand by an undiscriminating public, and in itself illustrates something of the problem confronting an author like Hardy, who apparently felt the expediency or necessity for serial publication, I yield to the temptation to quote the last paragraphs:

When Porter found himself again in his own room at Thames View, he sat down to write a note to Ellen and this time he addressed her as "My darling" without hesitation, and finished by calling himself "Your own." It was a short note and told briefly, in the simple language of the heart, the story of his and her great joy. He kissed it again and again and, encasing it in an envelope, confided the missive to the gardener with instructions to deliver it into Miss Somer's own hands. A golden coin ensured the man's absolute discretion and good-will.

Shortly afterwards, Ellen appeared. She was pale, but there was a smile of happiness and relief upon her face. Porter found immediate occasion to be near her. He guided her to one of the windows which opened on the lawn where the glorious view of garden, forest, field, and river, bathed in summer morning sunshine, extended before their eyes.

"You have received my note?" he asked.

"Yes," she whispered and looked at him as if her whole soul were alive with gratitude.

Her hand was hanging by her side. He took it in his own and bent over her.

"And may I ask now the question to which you could not listen yesterday?" he inquired.

She drooped her eyes and gently pressed his hand. He was answered and was happy.

A glance at *Harper's Magazine* for 1894 and 1895 (the time of *Jude the Obscure* as a serial), reveals much the same editorial conservatism, in fiction of a strictly conventional sort, and in articles on travel — sketches of a Norwegian winter, and of birds in the South Sea Islands.

Small wonder is it then that the story of the baptism of Tess's baby must not come out in the *Graphic*, or that *Harper's* readers must not know of Arabella's undisciplined capture of Jude. The former found publication, together with "For Conscience' Sake," a story based on illicit love and later published in *Life's Little Ironies* (1894), in the *Fortnightly Review*, that daring periodical, which could boast of a thoughtful public, and which in one year (July, 1891, to July, 1892), published two such iconoclastic articles as "The Emancipation of Women" and "Marriage and Free Thought." The last-named article, indeed, ventured to present the idea that adultery, instead of being an unpardonable offence, might instead be regarded as "merely a new experiment in living." [1]

But although Hardy's reasons for the alterations in the serial form of his stories seem easily established, and the alterations themselves more understandable in the light of the fiction in demand by the magazines in which these stories were published, the fact that such changes were made at all by an author of Hardy's position in the history of the English novel holds far deeper significance to the student of the novel in general and of Hardy's novels in particular. How far-reaching is that significance — in other words, how far are we justified in condemning Hardy's literary ethics? Such queries can best be satisfied by a brief consideration of his position in relation to other English realists of the nineteenth century.

To even a cursory student of the nineteenth century English novel, one fact is so obvious as to be axiomatic: that during that century, with the exception of the years during which Scott held sway, the novel was swept forward upon a rising tide of realism. That nineteenth century realism differed from that of the eighteenth century is also easily apparent, for in spite of the creation of such real characters as Parson Adams, Tom Bowling, Commodore Trunnion, Molly Seagrim, Squire Western, and Tom Jones, the novel of Smollett and of Fielding, even of Richardson, relied upon incident rather than upon character as the motivating force. Indeed, the progress of the novel from its earliest times has been a progress from incident to character, and not until the early years of the nineteenth century can it be said to have reached its goal.

With Jane Austen, however, character successfully defeats incident, and in such works as *Pride and Prejudice, Sense and Sensibility*, and *Emma* it is distinctly the motivating force. Moreover, in the hands of Miss Austen it was so successfully combined with plot — that is, with interdependent incidents — that in artistic method the novel left little to be desired. But it did need to be taken out of the parlor and made to face the facts of everyday existence in a world peopled with less fortunate souls than the Bingleys or the Dashwoods. In other words, the scope of its new realism, conceived and executed by Miss Austen, needed to be deepened and widened.

This was accomplished in different ways by the successors of Miss Austen, the great realists of the nineteenth century, Dickens, Thackeray, George Eliot, Meredith, Hardy. In the hands of Dickens, and influenced by philanthropic movements already on foot, the realistic novel took on a humanitarian aspect and centered its attention upon cruel schoolmasters, grasping lawyers, and thieves with children as accomplices, together with literally hundreds of other personages, who, exemplifying no particular abuse, live in the minds of thousands of readers, partly because of the humor of their portrayal, partly because within themselves they are the incarnation of some attribute of character. Grotesque exaggeration was the essence of Dickens' art in characterization, as it had been of Smollett's, and yet his men and women *are* real rather than romantic. In the almost scientific precision of his descriptive detail, in his mingling of comedy and satire, in placing the scenes of his stories in the workshop, the prison, the streets of London, and in his apparently pleasurable delineation of the humors of the vulgar, he has contributed largely to the realistic novel.

Thackeray's contribution, though not so large perhaps, is indisputable. True to his principle that he must accept the world as he found it, he depicted the social life in the vicinity of Bloomsbury and Russell Square, bringing to light its shams and hypocrisies, to be sure, with merciless satire, but not neglecting to recognize, together with its snobs and its climbers, its great and good characters. He pays always full deference to decorum, and is, like Dickens, strictly conventional in regard to matters of sex. Becky Sharp may have had intimate relations with Lord Steyne — in fact, we are left in no doubt that she did — but we are allowed to assume it only through the most conventional suggestion.

The breadth and sincerity with which George Eliot pictured English provincial life in its large aspects is in itself no small contribution to the realistic novel; and the debt of novelists and readers becomes larger when one remembers the sympathetic and accurate portrayals of such characters as Mrs. Poyser, the Gleggs and the Pullets, Dolly Winthrop, and Dinah Morris. But, more important still, the realistic novel in the hands of George Eliot makes a distinct advance over its predecessors in two particulars: First, in her contention that man is master of his own fate, that the act alone brings its train of good or ill, she introduces a system of philosophy into fiction; and second, in her fearless, if somewhat conventional, handling of love, irregular and illicit, which Thackeray and Dickens had touched upon so rarely, she paved the way for a greater consistency of characterization and a consequent broadening of the conception of realism.

It is not easy to catalogue Meredith's contribution to the realistic novel. Surely his conception of the novel was very like that of George Eliot: to her it was a vehicle for philosophic and ethical teaching; to him, for psychological and ethical. Both would depict the inner life by an exposure of character. But with the similar conception the similarity ends. Meredith did not believe in the realism that shows itself in minute and actual transcription of scene and of character. His realism, obscurely as it is often couched, has for its aim the depiction of types rather than of individuals, with the result that readers of his novels see in Sir Willoughby Patterne and Wilfrid Pole the allegorical figures of Egoism and of Sentimentalism. Meredith has no qualms as to the frank treatment of sex — it will be remembered that one of his pet contentions is that it is sentimentalism which determines the conduct of sex to sex — but his rambling, aphoristic, and at times almost unintelligible style would in itself preclude a strictly realistic or naturalistic scene which would presuppose drama in its execution. In consequence, though he deals candidly with such relations as are depicted between Dahlia Fleming and Edward Blancove, and again with the love of Matthew Weyburn for the Countess of Ormont, he gives us nothing approaching in dramatic intensity the scenes between Arthur Donnithorne and Hetty Poyser or many of those in the novels of Hardy.

Such were the tendencies of English realism in fiction up to and overlapping the time of the publication of *The Return of the Native* in 1878. In the hands of Dickens, Thackeray, George Eliot, Meredith, and others, the novel proved that it had taken the whole of human experience as its province, and if its authors had avoided the distinctly realistic treatment of certain issues, they had at least opened the door and cleared the way for a more daring successor.

This successor was Thomas Hardy. With him the nineteenth century novel was for the first time freed from the sentimental conventions of its predecessors and made the relentless exponent of every passion known to mankind; with him English realism became naturalism, not the minute and completely unrestrained naturalism of several of his French contemporaries, but a realism so far removed from anything that had gone before that it must needs be termed naturalistic in order to effect a satisfactory comparison.

Certain students of Hardy contend, it is true, that his realism is distinctly of French origin, but they give no grounds for such a contention, and there seems to be no basis for it other than the fact that there are certain similarities of treatment, which, to me at least, in view of Hardy's own realism, seem most natural and in themselves prove no definite influence.[3] Hardy as a matter of course must have known the works of Flaubert, the brothers Goncourt, Zola, and others; but we have at present no access to his correspondence, and in his few published articles there is no mention of any particular interest in the French writers of his day. His difference from the French is, it seems to me, greater than any similarity that there may be. In fact, because of certain unparalleled features of his art, distinctly his own, he stands away from and, indeed, above all the realists of his century, both English and French. The imagery of John Gould Fletcher, who in a *Yale Review* for 1920 sees Hardy as a great black rock off a long headland, standing high and alone at the full tide is, I think, not unsatisfying:

Off the long headland, threshed about by round-backed breakers,
There is a black rock, standing high at the full tide;
Off the headland there is emptiness,
And the moaning of the ocean,
And the black rock standing alone.

Like that of most novelists, Hardy's work is uneven, but there is evident in it, just as in the progress of the nineteenth century novel, an apparent, if sometimes interrupted, progress from incident to character, or from the more or less romantic view of life, tinged to be sure with realism, in *Desperate Remedies, Under the Greenwood Tree, A Pair of Blue Eyes*, and *Far from the Madding Crowd*, to the stark realism of the later novels. From *The Mayor of Casterbridge* (1886), the first novel considered in the foregoing study, to *Jude the Obscure* (1895) Hardy did not again forsake the realistic summit which he had first mounted with *The Return of the Native*.

And what are the qualities of his realism which makes that of other English novelists thin and superficial? What also are those unparalleled features of his art which set him in a place apart? The first and the greatest is his realistic conception of Nature, to appreciate which one may well look back for a moment to the treatment accorded to Nature by his realistic predecessors.

In Fielding, who "took the novel out-of-doors," and who deserves the title of the first English realist, Nature is absolutely detached from his characters or his plot, and his descriptions of natural scenery, relatively few in number, exist for themselves alone. Nature plays a decidedly negligible part in Miss Austen, Thackeray, and Dickens, and is still detached. In George Eliot, however, it begins to bear a definite relation to her characters and to the events of their lives. The best example of this treatment of Nature is shown, I think, in *The Mill on the Floss*, where the river from the beginning to the end of the story is, perhaps, the dominating influence in the life of Maggie Tulliver — indeed, of all at Dorlcote Mill — and symbolizes in its varying moods and in its never-ceasing, often tumultuous course the inconsistencies of Maggie's own experience and the relentless consequences of her reaction to life.

Again, in Meredith we have Nature presented in another aspect — as a source of righteousness and strength — a conception which is even more apparent in his poems than in his novels. Still it is clearly shown in *The Ordeal of Richard Feverel*, in the scenes where the storm speaks to Richard and sends him back to Lucy,[4] and where Diana feels her youth again among the Italian lakes and attributes the change to the "influence of beauty and grandeur." [5] Meredith's approach to life, however, is intellectual rather than emotional, and that very fact in itself precludes much of the sensuous treatment of Nature employed by the novelist whose approach is mainly emotional. It is interesting to note that the most memorable scenes in his novels are those idyllic and pastoral ones in his earlier works (notably *Richard Feverel* and *Sandra Belloni*) in which Nature is depicted as being in complete sympathy with those who read their own experience in her manifestations.

But in comparison with any or with all of these attitudes toward Nature, that of Hardy has a vastness of conception and of execution which was unknown in fiction before his time. In his novels Nature, in one form or another, is literally never absent. To attempt to interpret satisfactorily Hardy's conception and treatment is no easy task, and one that has offered ground for much contemplation and consequent disputation among critics. In my opinion, Nature is treated in three definitely different, but not necessarily inharmonious ways: First, Hardy portrays with amazing accuracy and almost scientific precision all the processes of Nature. Second, he constantly·stresses the inter-relation of man and Nature. Third, he depicts Nature, not as an abstraction, but as a vast, impassive organism living her own immense life and careless of that of man.

In the very earliest of the novels Hardy shows himself to be a tireless observer of the workings of Nature. His practical and exact knowledge is that of his Wessex shepherds, farm-laborers, and furze-cutters. His descriptions of the various sounds of the wind as it blows through different trees, and of the rain as it falls, now on the broad leaves of some plant, now on the ploughed earth, now on the road itself, are those of a scientist. In all his books there are passages that deal

with smells, sounds, color, with birds, sometimes asleep
at night as in *The Woodlanders* and *Tess*, with sheep
and cows, with ewes with their lambs in spring, with
fog over meadows and brush fires by night, with trees,
brooks, and flowers, with sowing and threshing, making cider, cutting swedes and furze.   No other English
novelist has added to the novel such poetry as this; no
other, except Shakespeare, says Mr. William Sharp, is
so distinctly English.[6]

In many of the novels, notably in *Far from the
Madding Crowd, Under the Greenwood Tree, The
Return of the Native, The Woodlanders*, and *Tess*,
man is seen again and again in his close relation to
Nature.   He is a part of her and she of him.   This
conception is beautifully illustrated by Clym Yeobright
in *The Return of the Native*, as he cuts furze in his
brown clothes on the brown stretches of Egdon Heath,
and by the other heath-dwellers as well, of whose lives
sombre Egdon is the dominating force; by Giles Win-
terbourne in *The Woodlanders*, out of sight among the
leaves of the great tree by Marty South's door, and by
Hardy's description of him as "Autumn's own brother"
after he has been at the cider-press.   Such men as Giles,
Clym Yeobright, Gabriel Oak, Dairyman Crick, and
the Yalbury farmers in *Under the Greenwood Tree*
live close to earth, among the sights, sounds, and smells
of the natural world, and, permeated by the things of
Nature, they become a part of her and she of them.

Lastly in Hardy's conception of Nature she appears
as the vast, unfeeling Power that rules the world, and

is totally indifferent, if not hostile, to man's desires and struggles. Nothing so typifies that Power as the well-known description of Egdon Heath in *The Return of the Native*. Against the dull immensity of the heath its inhabitants are analogous in Hardy's suggestion to the insignificance of human struggle against the all-pervading and overpowering force of Nature. It is not difficult to see that from such a conception there is bound to follow the most tragic irony. Though man may be related to Nature through his very closeness to her, she can have no regard for him in his struggles. Indeed, in Hardy's grim philosophy, if he would escape tragedy, he will not struggle.

It is through this conception that one gains from Hardy an awful sense of the pathetic futility of all human effort in the face of the relentless impartiality of the laws of Nature, and it is needless to point out what tremendously realistic themes are engendered by such a philosophy.

The effect of Hardy's realism is greatly enhanced by the artistic and distinctly dramatic unity of his best novels, the second attribute of his art which, it seems to me, sets him apart from other English realists. His biographers and critics tell us — indeed, we may discover it for ourselves through allusions in his own works — that he has always had a passion for the great Greek dramas, especially for those of Sophocles, whose attitude toward life was clearly similar to that of Hardy, and that, in the execution of his novels, he took the drama as his model. It is interesting to note here that Hardy was among the very first adherents and admirers of Ibsen, who, when his plays were translated, and introduced on the English stage from 1889 to 1896, was the object of the most bitter denunciation by leading periodicals and critics. Hardy, Meredith, and George Moore were the first members of the Independent Theater Association, which in 1891 sponsored the erection of a theater for the production of Ibsen's plays.[7] Three great realists lending moral support to a greater!

Unquestionably Hardy's knowledge of the drama influenced the technique of his novels, but there was another and a greater influence. Hardy was by taste and training an architect, and that training served him well as a novelist. *The Return of the Native* is a model of architectural skill in its perfect unity of time and place, its closely-woven and interdependent incidents, its rise of dramatic intensity; and *Tess* and *Jude*, though epical rather than dramatic in method, are alike examples of an enviable mastery of technical skill.

Flaubert once said of Pickwick: *"Quelle composition défectueuse! Tous les écrivains anglaise en sont là: Walter Scott excepté, ils manquent de plan."* If he had known Hardy, he would have added another and greater exception, for Hardy has unquestionably produced the most perfectly formed novels in our literature.

That this perfection of form was an ideal of his he tells us himself in an article entitled "The Profitable

Reading of Fiction," and published in the *Forum* for March, 1888.

"There is an æsthetic training," he says, "insensibly given by familiarity with a story which, presenting nothing exceptional in other respects, has the merit of being well and artistically constructed. To profit of this kind from this especial source, very little attention has hitherto been paid, though volumes have been written upon the development of the æsthetic sense by the study of painting and sculpture. Probably few of the general body denominated the reading public consider in their hurried perusal of novel after novel that, to a masterpiece in story, there appertains a beauty of shape, no less than to a masterpiece in pictorial or plastic art, capable of giving to the trained mind an equal pleasure."

The third and last quality of Hardy's art which gives him superiority over other English realists is, I think, the supreme consistency of his characterization. His men and women react to life in the only way they can — given always their environment and their heredity — and Hardy does not shrink from tracing their tragedies if consistency demands it. Nothing but tragedy can rightly follow such characters as Eustacia Vye, Michael Henchard, and Jude Fawley, and Hardy has no palliative for us. Nor is anything but tragedy consistent with the circumstances which baffle and finally overcome Tess Durbeyfield. The great test of sincerity and consistency in characterization is simply a sense of the inevitability of it all when the book is laid aside, and it is but fair to say that our greatest novelists rarely have failed the test. Hardy never fails it. Not only is he unhampered by the "happy ending" theory which dominates so many novelists even of the rank of Dickens, but the chain of his incidents goes relentlessly onward from the very beginning, even when, as is so apparent in *The Mayor*, *Tess*, and *Jude*, it is binding the victim with no hope of escape. Moreover, Hardy does not allow any deference to convention to eliminate from his pages scenes dealing with any phase of human passion if he thinks that scene necessary to the consistency of his characterization. If an Arabella Donn is to be depicted, then the motivating impulse of her life and nature must be depicted also.

These three attributes of Hardy's realistic art — his conception of Nature, the artistic and dramatic unity of his greatest novels, and his overwhelming consistency of characterization — place him, in my opinion, above all preceding or contemporary English realists. And it is in the light of that high position that one must consider the significance of the bowdlerizing of his novels for serial publication, since he has sacrified those very ideals of his art which have made him pre-eminent.

How he has belied his own philosophy of life, his conception of the irony and futility of human effort against the Power that rules the world, has already been shown in the preceding chapters. For what note of tragic irony is struck when Tess sees Angel Clare at the hotel in Sandbourne, since she has never given herself to Alec D'Urberville; or when Jude Fawley marries Arabella Donn, whom he despises, merely to get ahead of another lover? How he has marred the artistic and dramatic unity of at least two of his novels is evidenced in *Tess of the D'Urbervilles* by the omission from the serial of two entire chapters, and those the most dramatic (the one dealing with the seduction in The Chase and the other with the baptism of Sorrow), and in *The Well-Beloved* by the sacrifice of structure to melodrama in the serial and by an absurd and decidedly inferior handling of plot.[8] Finally, one has but to recall the tremendous sacrifice of consistency in the serial depiction of Alec D'Urberville, Jude Fawley, and Arabella Donn, and he will, I fear, be tempted to laugh up his sleeve at the enthusiastic approbation of the critics:

In Mr. Hardy . . . we have a man who puts the trivial and oft-repeated surface tricks behind him, who will stoop to nothing which he knows to be insignificant because he knows it will please, . . . who has a priestly adhesion to all that is best in the traditional ritual of letters.[9]

There is no courting of the popular taste in Mr. Hardy.[10]

Mr. Hardy is entirely uncompromising. He will not placate an audience. He offers no current, obvious views of life. He chooses his setting and abides in and by it.[11]

Hardy in *Tess* has revolutionized English fiction. A monumental work — marks a distinct epoch in English fiction. It bears the hall-mark of Truth on every page of it.[12]

And Mr. Hardy's own statement upon being presented with the gold medal of the Royal Society of Literature on the occasion of his seventy-second birthday sounds ironical in view of the preceding investigation; for in his speech of acceptance, given in abstract form in an article in the *Nation* for 1912 (vol. 94, p. 608), he "clearly indicates the need of appealing to the conscience and artistic honor of the literary craftsman."

Deeper than the joy of rapid production or of ephemeral popular appreciation is the satisfaction which springs from good work. The writer must somehow be got to put an ideal before him, and to labor incessantly for at least some approximation of it. Inner joys must be put above any species of outward reward if we are really to get the genuine and lasting motive for the production of good writing.

It may be that Hardy had found the seventeen years between the publication of *Jude the Obscure* and his speech of acceptance a season "meet for repentance"!

Were his attitude frankly that of his contemporary Anthony Trollope, who put novel-making upon a par with house-painting or horse-shoeing, and who wrote novels by the yard or by the job to suit his customers, his sole enthusiasm being for the cash that lay at the end of his literary labors, we should be justified in no criticism, at least as to the consistency and sincerity of his viewpoint. But in his own words, and in those of his biographers and critics, not to mention the proof evinced by his greatest novels, he is more than a literary craftsman; he is an artist with a mighty theory of his art — that of its adherence to the Truth. And it is from this eminence that he has descended to please and placate a reading public for whose taste and judgment he has only disdain, and whom he terms "the mentally and morally warped of both sexes, who will, where practicable, so twist plain and obvious meanings as to see in an honest picture of human nature an attack on religion, morals, or institutions." [13]

Amid the storm of criticism which burst in both England and America upon the publication of *Jude the Obscure*, only one reviewer seems to have grasped the irony of Hardy's theory in the light of his practice, and he has obscured his point in the vehemence of his attack on the indecency of the story. He writes:

> One circumstance we feel compelled to mention in order to give a finishing blow to the theory that Mr. Hardy's art, such as it is, is disinterested and sincere. When the story appeared as a serial in *Harper's*, it was a comparatively decent work. The author had studiously eliminated the most outrageous of his lubricities. In producing it as a book, he carefully sifts in the omitted filth, supplies the *lacunae* with the necessary filling, and sends it forth with all its present rancid revelations. In other words he furnishes a mild article for the family magazine and a highly spiced one for the *dura ilia* of the general public. Is this the attitude of a great literary artist with a single and consistent theory of the art? Is it not rather the canny suppleness of the smug peddler who with equal indifference vends a child's primer or brings out with a knowing leer a bundle of flash stories? [14]

It is not easy for the disciples and admirers of Hardy to accept this charge. The creator of *The Return of the Native, Tess*, and *Jude* a smug peddler! One rises to the defense, and then, as always when guilt has been already proved, intrenches himself behind the assertion that guilty though Hardy may be, he is no worse, for instance, than George Meredith, who published *Diana of the Crossways* in periodical form with the omission of the last ten chapters, and who left out chapters of *One of Our Conquerors* that it might be passed through the *Fortnightly Review* in seven issues.   But there is a distinct difference.   Meredith, though he shamelessly cut his novels to fit the space demands of the periodical editor, did not milk-feed the public by omitting or mutilating his greatest scenes until they became absurdities, and by rendering his greatest characterizations so inconsistent as to inspire the ridicule of even a cursory reader.   Moreover, Meredith's practice cannot be used to clear Hardy other than in the sense that the comparison proves them both culpable of a lack of respect for literary technique, for Meredith has no scenes which would distinctly harm the morals of the magazine reader, though they might exhaust his patience and puzzle his intellect.

George Moore is more akin to Hardy in his treatment of matters of sex, as well as in his feeling that "all things that live are to be pitied." [15]   Did he publish *Esther Waters* and *Evelyn Inness* serially?   He did not.   Moreover, in the preface of the American edition of the former he expresses a fine disdain for the attitude of a certain gentleman connected with the publishing house, who defended his contention that a certain passage dealing with the opera might arouse the sensual in his readers on the ground that it would take away subscriptions from the new opera-house! [16] Can one imagine Flaubert bowdlerizing *Madame Bovary*? — he, who after his novel was finished announced his intention of beginning at the first chapter and polishing every word and phrase?

Still we must guard against over-severity. We have no access at present to the correspondence of Hardy, nor do we know the material circumstances governing his life as a novelist. We do know that he was born to no competence and that in his early years he was an architect's apprentice. It is not likely that he was particularly well-to-do in 1871, at the time he published his first novel, *Desperate Remedies*, an undertaking which he himself financed, advancing seventy-five pounds for that purpose.[17] Upon the publication of *Far from the Madding Crowd* in 1874 his fame as a novelist seems to have been assured, but we have no record as to his financial success.

It would seem hardly possible, though in 1890 he does term himself a "representative of Grub Street," [18] that after a successful literary career of over ten years he would be suffering financial stress sufficiently severe to *demand*, in 1886 and thereafter, the serial publication (and with it the necessary bowdlerizing) of his novels, had he not wished to run them serially before their publication in book form. (One critic suggests that the very alteration of *Tess* was a tremendous advertisement for the novel in book form, as the magazine public upon hearing that there had been alterations and omissions in the *Graphic* version of the tale were eager to read the book itself and discover of what they had been cheated!)[19]

But having studied his position in the light of his predecessors and contemporaries and accorded him a place pre-eminent among English realists, we can do little more in closing than to allow him to speak for himself, defend his own case, and, it may be in these days of crass materialism, quite clear his own name from any smirch placed upon it.

In his article on "Candour in English Fiction," he suggests in his first sentence the problem facing him. "Even imagination," he says, "is the slave of stolid circumstance." In the paragraphs following he lays bare the situation as he sees it. On the one hand is the English reading public, which he characterizes in the preface of *A Laodicean* as "the comfortable ones whose lines have fallen unto them in pleasant places," "who have not yet reached ripeness of years," and which, he says in this article, "opposes a well-nigh insuperable bar to the treatment of catastrophes based upon sexual relationship." On the other is the fact that two popular vehicles have grown to be the media through which a novel can be successfully introduced to the public: the magazine and the circulating library. Both are controlled by this same reading public, which insists upon false views for the reading of young people; consequently, neither fosters the growth of the realistic novel. This situation, Hardy contends, "is not the fault of the authors, but circumstances over which they, as representatives of Grub Street, have no control."

I conclude this study with his own more definite statement of his position in the same article, which, it must be remembered, was written in 1890 before the serial publication of *Tess* and *Jude*:

In a ramification of the profounder passions the treatment of which makes the great style, something unsuitable is sure to arise; and then comes the struggle with the literary conscience. The opening scenes of the would-be great story may, in a rash moment, have been printed in some popular magazine before the remainder is written;[20] as it advances month by month the situations develop, and the writer asks himself, what will his characters do next? What would probably happen to them, given such beginnings? On his life and conscience, though he had not foreseen the thing, only one event could possibly happen, and that, therefore, he should narrate, as he calls himself a faithful artist. But, though pointing a fine moral, it is just one of those issues which are not to be mentioned in respectable magazines and select libraries. The dilemma then confronts him, he must either whip and scourge those characters into doing something contrary to their natures, to produce the spurious effect of their being in harmony with social forms and ordinances, or, by leaving them alone to act as they will, he must bring down the thunders of respectability upon his head, not to say ruin his editor, his publisher, and himself.

What he often does, indeed can scarcely help doing in such a strait, is belie his literary conscience, do despite to his best imaginative instincts by arranging a *dénouement* which he knows to be indescribably unreal and meretricious, but dear to the Grundyist and subscriber. If the true artist ever weeps, it is probably then, when he first discovers the fearful price that he has to pay for the privilege of writing in the English language — no less a price than the complete extinction, in the mind of every mature and penetrating reader, of sympathetic belief in his personages.

Were the objections of the scrupulous limited to a prurient treatment of the relations of the sexes, or to any view of vice calculated to undermine the essential principles of social order, all honest lovers of literature would be in accord with them. All really true literature directly or indirectly sounds as its refrain the words of the *Agamemnon*: "Chant Aelinon, Aelinon! but may the good prevail!" But the writer may point the *not* of his broken commandment in capitals of flame; it makes no difference. A question which should be wholly a question of treatment is confusedly regarded as a question of subject.

NOTES

[1] *Fortnightly Review*, vol. 56 (Old Series), vol. 50 (New Series), "Marriage and Free Thought."

[2] See the *Critic*, vol. 9, p. 19, and the *Gentleman's Magazine*, vol. 49, p. 321.

[3] Samuel C. Chew, in his recent study of Hardy (*Bryn Mawr Notes and Monographs*) sees the influence of Flaubert's *Emma Bovary* in the creation of Eustacia Vye. In fact, he terms Eustacia "a more passionate Emma Bovary." I cannot see the influence. Neither can I find any passage in *Madame Bovary*, which, as he claims, may have influenced Hardy in his description of Alec D'Urberville, the barn preacher.

[4] *The Ordeal of Richard Feverel* (Scribner edition, 1915), pp. 423-427.

[5] *Diana of the Crossways* (Scribner edition, 1915), p. 145.

[6] See the *Forum*, vol. 13, p. 583, "Thomas Hardy and His Novels."

[7] See Miriam Franc, *Ibsen in England* (Boston, 1919).

[8] In my Master's thesis, which was a comparative study of *The Well-Beloved* in serial and in book form, I pointed out that the structure of the serial was distinctly inferior to that of the book for the reason that the natural book divisions have been sacrificed for the sake of melodrama. I also showed that the serial plot lacks unity in comparison to that of the book, in that in the former there is no inter-

relation or inter-dependence of the characters, whose sudden appearance is dramatic but absolutely unmotivated. In the book, however, the plot is more closely knit and the dramatic unity assured.

[9] Edmund Gosse, "The Historic Place of Mr. Meredith and Mr. Hardy," in *International Review*, vol. 4, pp. 299-323.

[10] Lionel Johnson, *The Art of Thomas Hardy*, p. 231.

[11] Louise Willcox, "Thomas Hardy and His Novels," in *North American Review*, vol. 201, pp. 423-429. (I have taken the liberty of changing the tenses in this quotation.)

[12] *Westminster Review*, vol. 145, p. 136.

[13] "Candour in English Fiction," in *New Review*, January, 1890.

[14] "Jude the Obscure," in the *Bookman*, January, 1896.

[15] See the preface to the American edition of *Esther Waters*.

[16] *Ibid.*

[17] See the letter from Hardy to his publishers in Edward Newton's *The Amenities of Book-Collecting*, p. 12.

[18] "Candour in English Fiction," in *New Review*, January, 1890.

[19] "Is Thomas Hardy Overestimated?" in *Current Literature*, September, 1907.

[20] This reference is probably to *The Mayor of Casterbridge*, which was published serially in 1886, and which was the one novel nearest to 1890 that had been distinctly altered for serial publication.

A SELECTED BIBLIOGRAPHY OF BOOKS AND ARTICLES ON THOMAS HARDY

BOOKS

ABERCROMBIE, LASCELLES, *Thomas Hardy: A Critical Study.* (Martin Secker, 1912.)

BEACH, JOSEPH WARREN, *The Technique of Thomas Hardy.* (University of Chicago Press, 1922.)

CHEW, SAMUEL, *Thomas Hardy.* (*Bryn Mawr Notes and Monographs,* III, 1921.)

CHILD, HAROLD, *Thomas Hardy.* (Nisbet, 1916.)

GRIMSDITCH, HERBERT B., *Character and Environment in the Novels of Thomas Hardy.* (London: H. F. & G. Witherby, 1925.)

HEDGCOCK, F. A., *Thomas Hardy: Penseur et Artiste.* (Hanchette, 1911.)

JOHNSON, LIONEL, *The Art of Thomas Hardy.* (London: John Lane, 1895.)

MAGAZINE ARTICLES

ABERNETHY, J. W., "The Invasion of Realism," *Education,* 21: 469-474.

ARCHER, WILLIAM, "Real Conversations: II, with Mr. Thomas Hardy," *Critic,* April, 1901.

BARRIE, J. M., "Thomas Hardy," *Contemporary Review,* 56: 57.

BENSON, A. C., "Realism in Fiction," *North American,* 195: 820-832.

BINYON, LAURENCE, "The Art of Thomas Hardy," *Bookman* (London), February, 1915.

BOURGET, PAUL, "Limits of Realism in Fiction," *Living Age,* 196: 737.

BUTLER, A. J., "Mr. Hardy as a Decadent," *National Review,* May, 1896.

DOUGLAS, SIR GEORGE, "Some Critics of *Jude the Obscure,*" *Bookman,* January, 1896.

GOSSE, EDMUND, "The Historic Place of Mr. Meredith and Mr. Hardy," *International,* September, 1901.

——— ———, "Thomas Hardy," *Speaker,* September 13, 1890.

GREENWOOD, FREDERICK, "The Genius of Thomas Hardy," *Illustrated London News*, October 1, 1892.

HANNIGAN, D. F., "Mr. Thomas Hardy's Latest Novel," *Westminster Review*, 145:136.

Moss, M., "The Novels of Thomas Hardy," *Atlantic Monthly*, 98:354.

PARKER, W. M., "The Genius of Thomas Hardy," *Nineteenth Century*, 88:63-71.

SAPIR, E., "Realism in Prose Fiction," *Dial*, 63:503-506.

SHARP, WILLIAM, "Thomas Hardy and His Novels," *Forum*, 13:583-593.

STEVENSON, R. L., "Realism," *Critic*, 18:129.

STEWART, H. L., "Thomas Hardy as Teacher of His Age," *North American*, 208:584-596.

TYRRELL, R. Y., "Jude the Obscure," *Fortnightly Review*, 65:857.

WATSON, WILLIAM, "Tess of the D'Urbervilles," *Academy*, 41:125.

WILLCOX, L. C., "Thomas Hardy and His Novels," *North American*, 201:433-439.

ANONYMOUS ARTICLES

"Mr. Hardy's Novels," *British Quarterly*, 73:342-360.

"Is Thomas Hardy Overestimated?" *Current Literature*, September, 1907.

"The New Realism," *Living Age*, 212:564.

"The English Novel and Mr. Hardy," *Living Age*, 270:650.

"Realism," *Westminster Review*, 158:338-346.

MA
0